P9-AFE-573

Contemporary COOKING

Volume 7

BREAD

Contemporary COOKING

Volume 7

3M

Contemporary Cooking

Editorial production by James Charlton Associates, Ltd., New York. Editor-in-Chief, James Charlton; Executive Editor, Cara DeSilva; Managing Editors, Barbara Binswanger, Jennie McGregor; Food Editors, Helen Feingold, Inez M. Krech, Betsy Lawrence, Anne Lanigan, Maria Robbins, Joan Whitman.

**Book production and manufacturing consulting by:
Cobb/Dunlop Publishing Services, Inc., New York
Art Direction and interior design by:
Marsha Cohen/Parallelogram
Cover design by: Koechel/Peterson Design, Minneapolis**

Acknowledgments: Pat Cocklin, Delu PAL International, Alan Duns, John Elliott, Gus Francisco Photography, Melvin Grey, Gina Harris, Anthony Kay, Paul Kemp, David Levin, David Meldrum, Roger Phillips, Nick Powell, Iain Reid, John Turner, Paul Williams, George Wright, Cuisinarts, Inc.

Printed and bound in Yugoslavia by CGP Delo.

Library of Congress Cataloging in Publication Data
Main entry under title:

Contemporary Cooking.

Includes index.
1. Cookery. I. Minnesota Mining and Manufacturing Company.
TX715.C7586 1984 641.5 84-2563
0-88159-500-4 — (set)
ISBN: 0-88159–006–1

CONTENTS

for the Contemporary Cooking Series

VOLUME 7

Part One
SUMMER SOUPS

> "After the first ineffable *gazpacho* was served to us in Málaga and an entirely different and exquisite one was presented in Seville, the recipes for them had unquestionably become of greater importance . . . than cathedrals and museums. . . . Cook-books without number . . . were offered for inspection but not a *gazpacho* in any index. Oh, said the clerk, *gazpachos* are only eaten in Spain by peasants and Americans. . . .
>
> "At Cordoba there was another and suaver *gazpacho,* at Segovia one with a more vulgar appeal . . . Upon the return from Spain my host at Cannes, a distinguished Polish-American composer, a fine gourmet and experienced cook, listened to the story of the futile chase for *gazpacho* recipes, for their possible ingredients. Ah, said he, but you are describing a *chlodnik,* the Polish iced soup. Before he had had time to prepare it for us a Turkish guest arrived and he, hearing about the *gazpachos* and the *chlodnik* said, You are describing a Turkish *cacik.* . . . But that was not the end. There was the Greek *tarata.* Yes indeed, it was confusing."
>
> –Alice B. Toklas
> *The Alice B. Toklas Cook Book*

Although Miss Toklas penned these musings not that long ago (her charming cookbook was published in 1954), it is easy to see how times have changed, especially in culinary matters. The recipe for almost any dish, from almost every country in the world, can easily be found today. We have become quite international in our approach to cooking and to food. Miss Toklas might have been further surprised to discover the existence of *botvinya,* a cold herb soup from Russia, which includes sorrel and young beet tops among its many ingredients; *okrochka,* also from Russia and the Ukraine, a soup based on buttermilk that includes cucumbers, shrimps and dill; and many others, some traditional, some new, all following the basic principle of using the bountiful produce of summer to make a tempting, cooling soup.

These summer soups require little, if any, cooking. They are essentially liquid salads. Vegetables, herbs and other cooked ingredients—a hard-cooked egg, chicken or veal or beef, perhaps some shrimps—are moistened with enough liquid to turn a would-be salad into soup. The type of liquid varies with each country and each recipe; olive oil, lemon juice and tomato juice are dominant in most *gazpacho* recipes. Other cold soups rely on yogurt, buttermilk, sour cream or chicken stock.

In Russia, Poland, Hungary and other Eastern European countries, and all over Scandinavia as well, fruit soups abound in summertime. These can be glorious, rich with the fragrance of sun-ripened fruit, shimmering with sparkling color to rival any jewel. Fruit soups are made from cherries, strawberries, melons, raspberries, plums, blueberries, blackberries, apples, gooseberries, boysenberries and peaches. Many are garnished with lemons, limes, oranges. Fruit soups have never gained the same popularity in this country and this is a shame, for there are fewer more delicious or refreshing ways to tempt a summer palate.

Vegetable purée soups and velvety smooth cream soups form yet another category of iced summer soups to keep the heat away. One of the most famous of these is the suave and elegant vichyssoise, the origins of which seem to be a subject of perpetual dispute among culinary historians. Some claim that it is a purely American creation, first served at the Ritz-Carlton Hotel in New York City in 1910. The hotel's inventive chef was the famous Louis Diat, but his innovativeness in this case may have been limited to the idea of serving the traditional French leek and potato soup chilled. Whatever the origins, the result is wonderfully delicious and the basic idea lends itself to many variations: consider cold watercress and potato soup; spinach and potato soup; even arugula and potato soup.

Creative chefs are guided by the quality and quantity of produce in the marketplace. Fresh peas cooked briefly, puréed, and then enriched with cream are very good indeed served cold and garnished with a sprig of mint. Fresh mushrooms make an unusual and tasty summer soup; ripe avocados, asparagus, broccoli, cucumber and zucchini—all are the basis of refreshing summer soups.

The classic Billi Bi, which Craig Claiborne says "may well be the most elegant and delicious soup ever created," is excellent served cold. It is a rich and sumptuous combination of shelled mussels, herbs, spices and white wine, all bound together with a liaison of egg yolk and heavy cream. Served with a loaf of homemade bread, it is a meal unto itself.

Cold soups are usually served during the height of summer, when they are welcomed as a boon both to the diner and the cook, but there are times when it is good to break with custom and culinary cliché. A cold, well-seasoned soup, served as a prelude to a cozy winter meal, can also lift the spirits and transform an ordinary dinner into one that lingers in the mind and is recalled with interest and pleasure.

SUMMER SOUPS

Vegetable Purée Soups

These soups are made from one or more vegetables combined with the liquid in which they are cooked. Ingredients are reduced to a purée, using a food processor, blender, food mill or sieve. The resulting purée is as is, usually substantial enough to serve as a cold soup, and needs no thickening agent in the form of a roux or egg and cream liaison.

It is important to use fresh vegetables but, because the vegetables are reduced to a pulp, they may be slightly overripe or portions of foods that might otherwise go to waste, such as the outer leaves of lettuce, slightly tough end-of-season peas, watercress stems or mushroom peel. You can make delicious soups using a single vegetable or a judicious mixture of several kinds.

Tubers, such as potatoes and Jerusalem artichokes, make a thick soup after cooking and puréeing, as do root vegetables such as carrots, parsnips and turnips, and dried peas, beans and lentils.

Vegetables such as asparagus, celery, cucumber, lettuce, mushrooms, onions, spinach, tomatoes and watercress have less substance and a larger water content. If used alone, very large amounts would be needed to give the right consistency for a purée soup. An additional starchy vegetable, such as a potato, is usually added to thicken the soup.

Stock is probably the most frequently used liquid. Chicken and other white stocks are most suitable because strong brown stocks can overpower the flavor of the vegetable. By all means use vegetable stock where suitable. For example, for pea soup you can, if you like, use stock made from the pea pods.

Reserved vegetable cooking water may be used as a liquid base. Taste it first to be sure that the flavor is not too strong or too salty, as either could ruin a delicate soup. The water in which a cauliflower has been cooked, for instance, makes a valuable addition to cauliflower or parsnip soup.

Milk can be used, either by itself or combined with other liquids.

Preparing Vegetable Purées. Wash and trim all vegetables and, if necessary, peel them. There is no need to peel vegetables that are to be sieved or put through a food mill. Slice or chop the vegetables into rough pieces; it does not matter what size the pieces are. Next, simmer the vegetables in the liquid, be it stock or milk.

There are several ways to purée the soups. They can be poured through a conical sieve, the pulp being pressed through the sieve with a wooden pestle; this is the most work but gives very good texture.

A food mill, if it has a choice of plates (fine, medium, coarse), is probably the most versatile device because it can produce a variety of textures. A celery soup, for example, requires the fine plate to make it smooth, whereas turnip-and-cucumber soup is better if given a slightly coarser texture by milling the vegetables through the coarse plate. However, even if you have a food mill with a fixed plate, it is an excellent device. All seeds, peels and fibers will be trapped in the mill. To make a finer purée, the vegetables can be put through the mill twice.

Using a blender or a food processor fitted with the metal blade is undoubtedly the quickest and easiest way to reduce the vegetables to a purée. However, it may be necessary to sieve the soup after blending to remove fibers. Using an on-and-off pulse rather than long blending produces the slightly uneven texture desired for some purée soups.

Combination Soups. One vegetable alone makes a delicious soup, but a mixture of two or more can also be excellent; the addition of herbs and spices can improve both types. Here are a few ideas.

- Make a colorful soup from celeriac and tomatoes. Sieve the soup to remove tomato seeds and peel and celeriac fibers. Flavor with snipped chives and a little grated orange rind.
- Combine parsnip and apple and flavor with a little sage.
- Make a creamy soup from onion and cauliflower, and add a touch of color by flavoring and garnishing with paprika or grated nutmeg.
- Fresh sorrel leaves make a delicious, strongly flavored soup. Add a little potato to thicken the soup. Stir in a generous amount of light cream before serving.
- For *potage bonne femme,* a classic and economical French soup, use a mixture of leeks, carrots and potatoes, with a pinch of sugar to bring out the sweetness of the carrots.
- For a soup with delicate flavor and good color, use unpeeled zucchini and cook them in light chicken stock. Flavor with fresh chervil or dill.
- For Irish potato soup, simmer equal quantities of potatoes and onions in milk.
- For a quick tomato soup to rival gazpacho, crush a small garlic clove with salt. Purée in a blender or food processor with canned tomatoes and their liquid, a pinch of sugar, salt and pepper, and a good squeeze of lemon juice. Sieve after puréeing to eliminate tomato seeds.

Fruit Purée Soups

These soups are very popular in Scandinavian countries. Although they may seem strange to some tastes, they have a deliciously delicate flavor and can make a refreshing beginning or ending to a meal. Similar in method and texture to vegetable purée soups, fruit purée soups are made from fresh or dried fruits.

For best results with fresh fruits, be sure they are ripe. Apples, apricots, blackberries, cherries, melons, peaches, pears, plums, raspberries and strawberries can all be used. Of the dried fruits, apples, apricots, pears and prunes can be used successfully but pitted apricots and prunes give best results.

Making fruit soup rarely involves any cooking process other than poaching. Water, red or white wine, or a mixture of water and wine are the most commonly used liquids for poaching. Apple juice can be used in place of white wine. Chicken or beef stock is sometimes used, usually with apples.

Fruit soups made with a single fruit that has a high water content (apricots, cherries, plums) are frequently thickened with cornstarch or arrowroot. For a soup of medium thickness use approximately 1 tablespoon of cornstarch or 2½ teaspoons arrowroot per cup of liquid. This is added after the fruit has been cooked, but usually before puréeing. (Always dissolve either thickener in a small amount of cold water before using.) Remember, however, that the consistency of a soup to be served cold can be slightly thinner since the soup thickens on cooling. Many soups require no thickening at all.

If you are serving the soup as a first course, it may be flavored with nutmeg or mace, cinnamon, cloves, ginger, strips of lemon peel, and occasionally curry powder. Stir in fresh or sour cream or yogurt just before serving.

If you are serving the soup as a dessert, stir in sweetened whipped cream, or place a dollop on each portion, and sprinkle with grated nutmeg or ground cinnamon just before serving.

Preparing Fruit Purées. Wash and trim the fruit; peel, core, or pit as necessary. If you are puréeing the cooked fruit through a sieve or a food mill, leave the skins and pits of apricots and plums in the fruit as they will add extra flavor to the liquid and they will be separated out during puréeing.

Soak dried fruit overnight in the liquid to be used in the recipe.

Put prepared fruit in the saucepan and add the liquid and complementary flavoring. If both wine and water are used in the recipe, add only the water at

Cucumber Cream Soup

4 portions

½ small carrot
¼ celery rib
1 bay leaf
2 cups milk
3 ounces butter
2 tablespoons flour
salt and black pepper
pinch of grated nutmeg or mace
1 large cucumber
1 medium-sized onion
6 tablespoons heavy cream

- Use freshly ground white pepper for extra elegance.
- Small, garden-fresh zucchini can be substituted for the cucumber. Use 2 or 3 small ones, their total weight not much over 1 pound.
- Cucumber cream soup is very good served cold. Omit the final butter and chill in the refrigerator for several hours or overnight. Check seasoning before serving; cold soups often require more.
- Some snipped fresh dill would make an excellent garnish.

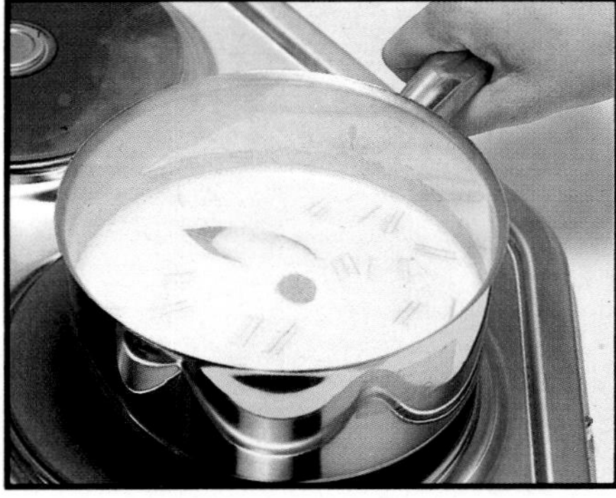

1 Prepare vegetables and place with bay leaf in the milk. Bring slowly to a boil, then cover and leave to cool for 30 minutes.

5 Melt 2 tablespoons of butter in a heavy saucepan over gentle heat. As soon as butter melts, add cucumber and onion.

9 Return soup to low heat. Taste and season lightly with salt and freshly ground pepper.

10 Measure cream into a small bowl. Spoon in about the same amount of hot soup and stir vigorously to mix well.

2 Make a roux with 1 ounce butter and the flour. Remove from heat and gradually stir in the milk drained from the vegetables.

3 Return pan to low heat and bring to a boil, stirring. Add salt and spices to taste, cover, and simmer for 10 minutes. This is a béchamel sauce.

4 Meanwhile, wash, dry, and chop cucumber. (Peel, only if waxed.) Peel and chop onion.

6 Cover pan and cook over gentle heat, shaking occasionally or stirring with a wooden spoon so vegetables cook evenly.

7 Add softened vegetables to béchamel sauce and simmer, covered, for 10 minutes so all flavors will infuse.

8 Purée vegetables and sauce in batches in a blender or food processor, or put through a food mill. Food processor is quickest.

11 Pour cream mixture into the remainder of the soup, whisking it in or stirring with a wooden spoon. Chill.

12 *To serve hot:* Reheat soup carefully but do not allow it to boil. Meanwhile, cut remaining butter into small pieces.

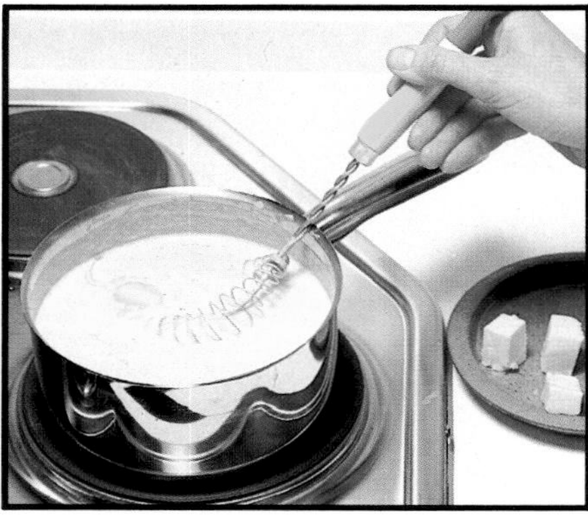

13 Add butter, 1 piece at a time, whisking or stirring it in, to give a final gloss. Adjust seasoning and serve.

Velouté Soups

1 If using vegetables that require parboiling, do this first. Drain and set aside.

2 If using fish, poach gently in stock or milk. Lift from cooking liquid with a slotted spatula. Reserve the liquid.

3 Set stock over low heat. Melt butter in a heavy pan over low heat.

OR If using celery, lettuce, mushrooms or a small amount of onion, sauté these in the butter, then stir in flour.

5 Remove pan from heat and pour in hot stock. Return to heat. Stir in drained parboiled vegetables or fish.

6 Season to taste. Bring to a boil, stirring, then lower heat and simmer, covered, until all ingredients are completely tender.

8 Purée the soup in a blender or food processor, or push through a sieve or food mill.

9 Return soup to low heat. Stir 2 tablespoons of hot soup into the egg-yolk and cream liaison to warm it.

10 Stir liaison into the soup. Simmer soup for 3 to 4 minutes, until it is thick, stirring all the time. Chill thoroughly.

4 Stir in flour to make a roux, and cook over low heat for about 3 minutes.

7 Prepare liaison of egg yolks and cream by whisking them together in a small bowl.

11 Serve soup in a tureen or in individual bowls with garnish or accompaniment.

the start. Wine is added after the fruit is partly poached or after it is puréed so that the wine is not simmered for a long time.

Bring liquid to the simmering point and simmer, covered, until ingredients are quite tender, from 10 to 25 minutes, depending on the fruit used.

With the exception of berries, purée fruits in the same way as vegetables, using whichever device you prefer. Only very fleshy berries such as strawberries can be puréed in a food mill. Smaller berries such as blackberries and raspberries have only a small amount of pulp, so purée these by sieving, or by puréeing in a blender and then sieving to remove seeds.

Before reducing the fruit to a purée, spoon off and reserve some of the liquid if you want to thicken the soup. Cool this portion of liquid, stir in the needed amount of cornstarch, then combine with the cooked fruit. Cook over low heat, stirring, until the soup is thickened. Do not make it too thick at this stage as it will become somewhat thicker as it cools. Cool and chill the soup.

Cream Soups

Cream soups are only one step up from the simple purée soup. They take longer to make, but you will find their delicious results worth the extra effort. However, these soups are not everyday fare; they are for occasions when you want to do something special for family or guests. They provide a contrast in flavor, texture and color to the following courses.

These soups are rich and creamy. The cream binds the ingredients to produce a smooth consistency and also makes the soup taste very rich. Most summer cream soups are vegetable-based, taking advantage of the variety of produce available in this season. Many need only cream to thicken them. The starch content of some root vegetables provides sufficient thickening so the ingredients can be simmered in milk or stock and made into a purée without needing the addition of béchamel sauce (see Volume 3 Index) or other thickener. In all cases the soup is enriched with a final addition of cream.

The vegetables should be fresh, but as with the simple purées you can make good use of vegetable trimmings such as green leek tops or the outer leaves of a lettuce head; even pea and bean pods make very good soups.

Almost any vegetable can be used to make a cream soup, apart from eggplant, which has a spongy texture and does not give good flavor. All leafy greens are suitable—lettuces, spinach, watercress. Green beans, leeks, mushrooms, peas, tomatoes, as well as all root vegetables, such as Jerusalem artichokes, make good cream soups.

The liquid, either for the béchamel sauce or for cooking the vegetables themselves, may be milk, stock or water. Generally milk is used for green leafy vegetables so that the vegetable flavor is not too strong and the color is suitably delicate. Chicken or white stock is used for other vegetables where its flavor will not overpower that of the main ingredients. A light vegetable stock may be used in the same way. Water may be used for tomato- and potato-based soups.

The rich flavor and smooth consistency of cream soups come from the final addition of cream. (In the case of hot soups, butter is added as well.) The cream should be fresh heavy cream; light cream will not give the same results.

Preparing Vegetable Cream Soups. To make cream soups with green leafy vegetables or other nonstarchy vegetables such as tomatoes or mushrooms, prepare a béchamel sauce. First infuse 2 cups milk with the flavorings. Then make a roux with 2 tablespoons butter and 2 tablespoons flour, strain the flavored milk into it, cover, and simmer for 10 minutes. This gives a sauce of pouring consistency.

Wash and trim the vegetables and chop or slice them. Melt about 2 tablespoons butter in a thick heavy saucepan. Add the vegetables, cover the pan, and cook very gently for 5 to 10 minutes, until most of the butter has been absorbed. Shake the saucepan or stir the ingredients occasionally to prevent sticking and to ensure even cooking.

Add the cooked vegetables to the saucepan containing the béchamel sauce. Add complementary herbs, cover the pan, and simmer over low heat for 5 to 10 minutes to infuse the flavor of the vegetables and herbs in the sauce. Purée the soup.

Now check the soup for consistency. It should have the consistency of light cream; if the soup is too thick at this point, thin it with a little stock or milk. The final addition of cream, as well as the chilling, will thicken it slightly.

A cream soup is enriched shortly before serving by the addition of heavy cream, which gives the soup its distinctive, rich, smooth and creamy taste.

Pour the cream into a bowl and stir or whisk in about 1/4 cup of the hot soup. Stir to mix thoroughly and to warm the cream. Pour this blended mixture into the balance of the soup in the saucepan. Stir or whisk the soup, using a wooden spoon or wire whisk, until blended. If you were to pour the cold cream directly into the hot soup, the cream could separate and the butterfat would disperse in small globules across the surface.

Allow the soup to cool to room temperature, for 30 to 40 minutes, then chill for at least 3 hours. (To serve the soup hot, reheat over moderate heat. Stir occasionally. Do not let it boil. If the soup were allowed to boil, the cream would curdle.)

Garnishes and Accompaniments. The pale color and smooth texture of cream soups lend themselves to crisp textures and strong colors in garnishes and accompaniments. Decorate just before serving with julienne strips of vegetables such as raw carrot, celery, green or red pepper, paper-thin slices of cucumber or small mushrooms, snipped chives, watercress sprigs, thin slices of lemon, or extravagant swirls of thick cream. Alternately, garnish with a few split almonds which have been sautéed in butter until golden brown (particularly good with green bean soups).

Velouté Soups

These soups are a simple advance on cream soups, so anyone who can make a cream soup will have no problems with this procedure. The same basic ingredients can be used but they are combined with a velouté instead of a béchamel. Velouté is made from stock cooked with a butter and flour roux. The thickening is an egg-yolk and cream liaison. The liaison is whisked together, warmed with some of the hot soup, then whisked into the rest of the soup, which is very slowly reheated. It is necessary to warm the liaison before adding it to the soup; otherwise the cold egg yolks would cook into egg threads when dropped into the hot mixture. The very slow reheating is also important, as it prevents curdling of the eggs.

After the liaison is added, bring the soup to a simmer and let it reach the point just below boiling, when a few bubbles appear at the surface. This cooks the egg yolks so that they do not cause the soup to liquefy later.

These soups look creamy and beautiful by themselves, but they can be served with garnishes—tiny pastry puffs, blanched or butter-steamed vegetable slivers, or watercress leaves.

Serving and Storing Cold Soups

The seasoning in cold soups should be rather stronger than you might expect, since our tastebuds experience chilled food as less flavorful. Cool the soup, cover, and chill thoroughly for about 3 hours before serving. Do not be tempted to speed up the chilling process by floating ice cubes in the soup; that would only dilute the flavors and make the soup watery.

Purée soups can be stored both in the refrigerator and in the freezer. When the soup has cooled, pour it into a container with an airtight lid, and cover. The soup will keep in the refrigerator for a maximum of 4 days.

For freezing, pour the cooled soup into ice-cube trays and freeze. Then empty the cubes into freezer bags, seal, and store in the freezer. Alternatively, pour soup into an airtight

Gazpacho

6 portions

2½ pounds very ripe tomatoes
2 garlic cloves
1 large cucumber
3 tablespoons olive oil
3 tablespoons fresh lemon juice
2 teaspoons minced fresh mint
4 teaspoons minced fresh parsley
Tabasco®
salt and black pepper

Garnishes

chopped mild onion
chopped green pepper
pitted black olives
toasted small croutons

4 **Use processor to chop separately the onion, green pepper and olives for garnish.**

1 Blanch and peel tomatoes. Peel garlic cloves and cucumber. Cut all into rough chunks.

2 Put vegetables, 2 cups at a time, into the bowl of a food processor fitted with the steel blade.

3 Purée vegetables; turn each batch into a large bowl; mix well. Stir in olive oil, lemon juice and herbs. Chill.

5 Put each garnish in a separate serving bowl and keep cold until time to serve the soup.

6 Remove soup from refrigerator. Thin, if necessary, with ice-cold water. Add Tabasco and salt and pepper to taste.

7 Serve soup very cold. Accompany with bowls of garnishes.

container, leaving ½ inch of head space, cover with the lid, and freeze. Either way, the soup should keep for up to 2 months.

Cream soups and velouté soups can also be stored in both refrigerator and freezer. The basic soups, without the enrichment of cream or liaison, may be kept in a covered container in the refrigerator for a day or two, or in the freezer for up to 2 months. Add the cream or the liaison after defrosting, and just before serving the soup.

If you are planning to freeze cream soups that are based on béchamel sauce, replace the flour in the sauce with cornstarch. This is because soups that are thickened with flour tend to curdle on reheating. Do not freeze soups that have a large amount of potatoes in them, because potatoes become slushy when frozen in a liquid.

If a soup recipe includes herbs and spices, it is best to leave these out until the soup is defrosted for use. This gives the soup a much fresher flavor.

No soup should be stored in the freezer for longer than 2 months because it will develop a sour taste.

Tomato Soup

4 portions

1½ pounds tomatoes
1 medium-size onion
rind of ¼ orange
2 tablespoons butter
3¾ cups chicken stock
1 bay leaf
½ teaspoon black pepper
¼ teaspoon salt
2 teaspoons lemon juice
1 teaspoon sugar

Blanch and peel the tomatoes and cut them into quarters. Peel and mince the onion. Pare off the orange rind, making very thin pieces with no white portion of the peel. Melt the butter in a medium-size saucepan over low heat. Add tomatoes and cook for 10 minutes, stirring frequently. Increase heat to moderate and add the stock, minced onion, bay leaf, pepper, salt and orange rind pieces. When the liquid comes to a boil, reduce heat to low, cover the pan, and simmer for 45 minutes.

Remove pan from heat and purée the soup in a food mill, blender or food processor. Add the lemon juice and sugar to the puréed soup and place soup over low heat. Bring it to a boil, stirring frequently. Remove pan from heat and let the soup stand at room temperature until cool. Chill.

Check seasoning before serving, and serve chilled.

Yogurt and Avocado Soup

4 portions

4 ripe avocados
juice of 2 lemons
½ teaspoon salt
½ teaspoon black pepper
2 teaspoons Worcestershire sauce
1¼ cups plain yogurt
¼ teaspoon cayenne pepper

Peel and halve the avocados and remove pits. Cut into pieces. Place avocados, lemon juice, salt, pepper and Worcestershire sauce in the jar of an electric blender or the bowl of a food processor. Blend at high speed for 30 seconds, until the mixture forms a purée. Transfer the purée to a large serving bowl or soup tureen and stir in the yogurt. Put the bowl or tureen in the refrigerator to chill for 30 minutes.

Remove bowl from refrigerator, sprinkle cayenne over the soup, and serve immediately.

Cucumber and Yogurt Soup

4 portions

1 small onion
1 large cucumber
1 tablespoon butter or margarine
2 cups chicken stock, or half milk, half stock
salt and black pepper
leaves of 1 large mint sprig
½ cup plain yogurt

Peel and chop the onion. Peel and slice the cucumber. Melt the butter in a heavy pan over low heat. Add onion and cucumber and sauté for 3 minutes. Pour in the stock. Season to taste and bring to a boil. Cool slightly. Add the mint leaves. Purée in a blender or food processor. Chill.

Just before serving, stir in the yogurt.

Turnip and Cucumber Soup

4 portions

8 ounces turnip tops
salt and black pepper
2 cups chicken stock (see Volume 1 Index)
1 medium-size cucumber
1 cup sour cream
2 teaspoons snipped fresh dill

Wash turnip tops. Put in a saucepan, season with salt and pepper, and pour in the stock. Bring to the simmering point, cover, and simmer for 20 minutes. Purée the soup in a food mill, blender or food processor. Peel cucumber and cut into thin slices. Stir slices into the purée. Cool, then chill the soup.

At serving time stir in the sour cream and sprinkle with fresh dill.

Curried Apple Soup

6 portions

1½ pounds apples
1 teaspoon lemon juice
1 small onion
3 cups chicken stock
½ teaspoon ground turmeric
½ teaspoon ground cuminseed
½ teaspoon ground coriander
pinch of ground cloves
salt
½ cup light cream
6 tablespoons plain yogurt

Peel and core the apples; reserve half of one apple for garnish. Brush cut surface of apple with ½ teaspoon lemon juice and cover with plastic wrap. Peel the onion. Chop remaining apples and the onion into small pieces. Put apples and onion in a saucepan, pour in 1½ cups of the stock, and add remaining lemon juice, spices, and salt to taste. Cover the pan and simmer for about 10 minutes, until apples are tender.

Purée the apple mixture in a food mill, blender or food processor. Stir in remaining stock. Cool the soup.

When soup is cold, stir in the cream and the yogurt, cover, and chill. Just before serving, stir in ½ cup cold water if the soup seems too thick. Check the seasoning and add more salt if necessary. Cut the reserved apple half into 12 paper-thin slices and garnish each portion with 2 slices.

Melon and Strawberry Soup

4 to 6 portions

- **8 ounces ripe melon**
- **8 ounces fresh strawberries**
- **2 tablespoons granulated sugar**
- **2 cups water**
- **1 lemon**
- **2 tablespoons cornstarch**
- **1½ cups white wine**

Cut the melon from the rind and discard seeds. Hull the strawberries. Slice both fruits. Place fruits in a medium-size saucepan with the sugar and water. Pare the rind from the lemon and add rind to the saucepan. Bring liquid to the simmering point, cover, and simmer for 20 minutes.

Mix the cornstarch and a little of the wine to a smooth paste. Stir the rest of the wine into the cornstarch mixture and then pour into the soup, stirring all the while. Cook slowly, still stirring, until soup comes to a boil and thickens slightly. Simmer for 5 minutes. Remove and discard the lemon rind. Purée the soup in a food mill, blender or food processor. Cool the soup, then chill it.

Pear-and-White-Wine Soup

4 to 6 portions

- **1 pound ripe pears**
- **2 tablespoons sugar**
- **2 cups water**
- **¼ teaspoon ground ginger**
- **1 lemon**
- **2 tablespoons cornstarch**
- **1½ cups white wine**

Peel and core pears and chop into rough pieces. Place pears in a medium-size saucepan with the sugar, water and the ginger. Pare the rind from the lemon and add to the saucepan. Bring to the simmering point, cover, and poach for 20 minutes.

Mix the cornstarch and a little of the wine to a smooth paste. Stir the rest of the wine into the cornstarch mixture and then pour into the soup, stirring all the while. Cook slowly, still stirring, until soup comes to a boil and thickens slightly. Simmer for 5 minutes. Remove and discard lemon rind. Purée the soup in a food mill, blender or food processor. Cool the soup, then chill it.

Hungarian Apricot Soup

4 portions

- **4 ounces dried apricots (⅔ cup)**
- **1¼ cups dry white wine**
- **4 ounces boned cooked chicken**
- **1 garlic clove**
- **2 tablespoons butter**
- **2 tablespoons flour**
- **2½ cups chicken stock**
- **1 tablespoon snipped fresh chives**
- **½ teaspoon salt**
- **¼ teaspoon black pepper**
- **⅛ teaspoon grated nutmeg**
- **¾ cup sour cream**

Soak the apricots in the wine for 6 hours. Dice the chicken. Peel and crush the garlic. Melt the butter in a large saucepan over moderate heat. Add the garlic and cook, stirring occasionally, for 4 minutes. Remove pan from heat. With a wooden spoon, stir in the flour to make a smooth paste. Gradually add the stock, stirring constantly. Stir in the apricots and wine, diced chicken, chives, salt, pepper and nutmeg. Set the pan over high heat and bring soup to a boil, stirring constantly. Reduce heat to low, cover the pan, and simmer the soup, stirring occasionally, for 30 minutes.

Remove pan from heat and cool the soup. Stir in the sour cream and chill. Check the seasoning before serving.

Fruit Soup

4 portions

2 pounds mixed fruits
¼ cup sugar
⅛ teaspoon salt
1 whole clove
1 cinnamon stick, 2 inches
juice and grated rind of 1 lemon
3 cups water

Wash and peel the fruits, and chop them. Place fruits in a large saucepan. Add the sugar, salt, clove, cinnamon stick and lemon juice and rind. Pour in the water and bring the mixture to a boil over high heat, stirring occasionally. Reduce heat to low, cover the pan, and cook the fruit for 10 to 15 minutes, until it is tender but still firm. Remove and discard the cinnamon stick and the clove.

Strain the soup into a large serving bowl, rubbing the fruit pulp through the strainer with the back of a wooden spoon or a wooden pestle. Discard any pulp that remains in the strainer; it will contain fibers. Set the soup aside to cool for 15 minutes. Place soup in the refrigerator to chill for 1 hour before serving.

Cream of Asparagus Soup

4 to 6 portions

1 pound asparagus
1 medium-size onion
2 tablespoons butter
3 tablespoons flour
5 cups hot chicken stock
½ teaspoon salt
¼ teaspoon black pepper
½ teaspoon celery salt
¼ teaspoon grated nutmeg
1¼ cups light cream

Wash asparagus, trim off scales, break off the tough bottom portion of each stalk, and peel stalks if necessary. Chop all the asparagus. Peel and mince the onion. Melt the butter in a saucepan over moderate heat. Add the onion and cook, stirring occasionally, for 5 to 7 minutes, until onion is soft and translucent but not browned. Remove pan from heat. With a wooden spoon, stir in the flour to make a smooth paste. Gradually stir in the chicken stock, being careful to avoid lumps. Stir in salt, black pepper, celery salt, nutmeg and the chopped asparagus.

Return pan to heat and bring the soup to a boil, stirring constantly. Reduce heat to low, cover the pan, and simmer, stirring occasionally, for 20 to 30 minutes, until the asparagus is very tender, including the thickest pieces of the stalks. Pour the soup through a fine wire strainer set over a mixing bowl. Using the back of a wooden spoon, or a wooden pestle, rub the asparagus through the strainer. Alternatively, purée the soup in a blender or food processor.

Stir the cream into the purée and pour the soup into a chilled soup tureen, or individual soup bowls. Cool the soup to room temperature, then chill in the refrigerator for 2 hours before serving.

Borscht

(Russian Beet Soup)

6 portions

12 ounces raw beets
salt
8 ounces green cabbage
1 medium-size onion
2 tablespoons butter
3 cups chicken stock
1 teaspoon caraway seeds
1 teaspoon sugar
black pepper
juice of 1 lemon
¼ cup dry white wine
6 tablespoons sour cream

Wash and trim beets, leaving at least 2 inches of stem on each beet. Cook the beets in boiling salted water for 40 to 50 minutes, until all are tender. Cool, then slip off the skins. Grate the beets by hand or in a food processor fitted with shredder blade, and reserve any juice.

Wash the cabbage and shred it. Bring 1 cup salted water to a boil in a saucepan. Add the cabbage, cover the pan, and simmer for 8 minutes.

Peel and chop the onion. Melt the butter in a large pan and cook, stirring occasionally, for 5 to 7 minutes, until onion is soft and translucent but not browned. Pour the chicken stock into the onion and bring stock to a boil. Add the cabbage and its cooking liquid, the grated beets and their juice, the caraway seeds, sugar, and salt and black pepper to taste. Simmer for 10 minutes, removing any foam from the surface with a slotted spoon or stock skimmer. Add the lemon juice and wine and bring to a boil. Check the seasoning. Purée the soup in a food mill, blender or food processor. Cool and chill the soup.

When ready to serve, add swirls of sour cream to the soup tureen or individual bowls.

Cream of Broccoli Soup

4 to 6 portions

12 ounces broccoli
12 scallions
2 large carrots
2 celery ribs
2 garlic cloves
1 bay leaf
1 teaspoon salt
½ teaspoon white pepper
½ teaspoon paprika
3¾ cups chicken stock
1 cup light cream
¼ cup sour cream

Wash broccoli, trim, and separate flowerets from stems. Peel stems if necessary and cut into small pieces. Cut the flowerets into larger pieces. Cook broccoli in boiling water for about 5 minutes, until tender but not mushy. Drain well and chop. (If unsauced, leftover cooked broccoli can be used for this soup.)

Wash and trim the scallions and chop both green and white parts. Wash and scrape carrots and cut into thin slices. Wash and dry celery, trim if necessary, and chop both ribs and leaves. Peel and crush the garlic cloves. Place the scallions, carrots, celery, garlic, bay leaf and 1 cup water in a large heavy saucepan. Set pan over moderate heat and bring the water to a boil, stirring constantly. Cover the saucepan, reduce heat to low, and simmer for 15 to 20 minutes, until vegetables are tender. Remove pan from heat and add the cooked broccoli, the salt, pepper, paprika and chicken stock; stir well. Return pan to heat and cook the soup, stirring constantly, for 10 minutes.

Pour the soup through a fine wire strainer set over a large mixing bowl. With the back of a wooden spoon, or a wooden pestle, rub the vegetables through the strainer. Discard any pulp or fibers remaining in the strainer. Alternatively, remove the bay leaf and purée the soup in a blender or food processor until the mixture is smooth.

Return purée to the saucepan and set over low heat. Stir in the light cream. Cook the soup, stirring constantly, for 5 minutes, until it is heated through. Remove pan from heat and cool the soup. Stir in the sour cream and chill. Check seasoning before serving.

Cream of Spinach Soup

4 portions

Béchamel Sauce

- **½ small carrot**
- **¼ celery rib**
- **2 cups milk**
- **1 bay leaf**
- **2 tablespoons butter**
- **3 tablespoons flour**
- **salt and white pepper**
- **pinch of grated nutmeg or mace**

- **1 pound fresh spinach**
- **4 tablespoons butter**
- **salt and black pepper**
- **6 tablespoons heavy cream**

Scrub and scrape the carrot, and wash and dry the celery. Chop both vegetables and place them in a saucepan. Pour in the milk and add the bay leaf. Bring slowly to a boil. Remove from heat, cover, and leave to infuse for 30 minutes. Strain and rewarm the milk. Make a roux with the butter and flour, remove from the heat, and stir the warmed milk into the roux. Return pan to low heat and bring to a boil, stirring. Season with salt and white pepper to taste and add nutmeg or mace. Cover and simmer for 10 minutes.

Meanwhile, wash the spinach thoroughly in several changes of room-temperature water. Drain, shake dry, and discard any tough stems or damaged leaves. Melt 2 tablespoons of the butter in a large saucepan over low heat. Add the spinach, cover, and sweat it for about 10 minutes, until leaves are limp; they should still be bright green. Shake the pan or stir frequently so the spinach cooks evenly and absorbs the butter without burning. Add the spinach to the béchamel sauce and simmer, covered, for 10 minutes. Purée the soup in a food mill, blender or food processor.

Return purée to the saucepan, taste, and season lightly with salt and black pepper. Reheat gently. Pour the cream into a small bowl and spoon in some of the hot soup. Stir vigorously to mix and warm the cream. Pour the cream and soup mixture into the balance of the hot soup, stirring all the time. Chill. Check seasoning before serving.

Variation: This soup can be made with 10 ounces frozen leaf spinach. For sorrel and spinach soup, replace half of the fresh spinach with sorrel leaves.

Cream of Lettuce Soup

4 portions

Velouté Sauce

- **2 tablespoons butter**
- **2 tablespoons flour**
- **2 cups chicken stock**
- **salt and white pepper**

- **2 medium-size heads of Boston lettuce or 4 heads bibb**
- **1 small onion**
- **2 tablespoons butter**
- **salt and white pepper**
- **6 tablespoons heavy cream**

Make the velouté sauce: Melt the butter in a saucepan and stir in the flour to make a roux. Warm the stock. Remove saucepan from heat and stir the stock into the roux. Return pan to low heat and bring to a boil, stirring. Season the sauce with salt and pepper. Cover and simmer for 10 minutes.

Meanwhile, wash and dry the lettuce; peel and mince the onion. Melt the butter in a saucepan and, stirring occasionally, gently cook the onion and lettuce for about 10 minutes, until both are soft. Add onion and lettuce to the velouté sauce and simmer, covered, for 10 minutes.

Purée the soup in a food mill, blender or food processor. Return soup to the saucepan, taste, and season lightly with salt and freshly ground white pepper. Pour the cream into a small bowl. Spoon some of the hot soup into the cream and stir vigorously to mix and to warm the cream. Pour the cream and soup mixture into the rest of the hot soup, stirring all the time. Reheat gently, but do not let the soup boil. Cool the soup, then chill it. Adjust the seasoning before serving.

Almond and Watercress Soup

4 to 6 portions

- 1 pound watercress
- 1 medium-size onion
- 1 garlic clove
- 4 ounces blanched almonds, ground
- 4 cups chicken stock
- ½ cup heavy cream
- salt and black pepper
- watercress leaves for garnish

Wash and drain the watercress and remove about half of the stems. Peel onion and garlic and cut into quarters. Place watercress, onion, garlic and almonds in a large saucepan and pour in the chicken stock. Bring to a boil and simmer gently for about 15 minutes, until onion is tender. Purée the soup in a food mill, blender or food processor. Stir the heavy cream into the purée. Add salt and pepper to taste. Cool the soup, cover, and chill for at least 3 hours.

Adjust seasoning before serving. Garnish each portion with watercress leaves.

Crème Vichyssoise Glacée

6 portions

8 ounces potatoes
2 large onions
1 large leek
2 tablespoons butter
3 cups chicken stock
salt and white pepper
1 cup heavy cream
6 tablespoons snipped fresh chives

Peel and chop the potatoes and onions. Wash the leek, remove and discard most of the green part, and chop the rest of the leek. Melt the butter in a saucepan and sweat the potatoes, onions and leek for 10 minutes, until all the vegetables are soft. Pour in the stock and simmer, covered, for 25 minutes, until the vegetables are very tender.

Purée the soup in a food mill, blender or food processor. Taste and season lightly with salt and white pepper. Cool the soup, then stir in the cream. Chill the soup for about 3 hours.

Just before serving, sprinkle the chives over the soup.

Variation: A nourishing soup can be made of watercress (which contains vitamins A and C and iron) and potato. Wash a large bunch of watercress, remove tough stems, and chop the rest. Reserve a few leaves for garnish. Peel and dice 1 pound potatoes. Continue as for vichyssoise, substituting watercress for leek. Garnish with reserved watercress leaves.

Green Pea and Lettuce Soup

4 portions

1 head of Boston lettuce
½ small onion
2 tablespoons butter
1½ cups chicken stock
8 ounces frozen peas
2 tablespoons flour
½ cup milk
salt and black pepper
2 large egg yolks
½ cup heavy cream

Wash and dry the lettuce. Chop into rough pieces. Peel and mince the onion. Melt the butter in a heavy saucepan over low heat. Warm the stock over low heat. Sauté the onion, lettuce and peas in the butter for 3 minutes. Stir in the flour and cook for 3 minutes longer. Remove pan from heat and pour in the warmed stock and the milk, stirring. Return saucepan to heat and bring soup to a boil, stirring. Reduce heat and cook, covered, for 5 minutes. Season to taste.

Meanwhile, beat the egg yolks and cream together. Purée the soup in a blender or food processor. Return the purée to the saucepan and again set over low heat. Stir about 4 tablespoons of the hot soup into the liaison of eggs and cream; mix thoroughly. Stir the warmed liaison into the balance of the soup. Simmer gently for 4 minutes, stirring all the time. Serve hot or chilled.

Purée of Fennel with Cream

4 portions

12 ounces fennel
2 cups water or chicken stock
salt and black pepper
1 cup heavy cream

Wash the fennel bulb; discard stems and any coarse outer portions. Reserve the ferny fronds for garnish. Chop the fennel bulb and place in a saucepan. Cover with water or stock and season with salt and pepper to taste. Cover the pan and simmer for about 15 minutes, until fennel is very tender.

Purée the fennel mixture in a food mill, blender or food processor. Cool the purée. When it is cold, stir in the cream, cover, and chill. Garnish with the reserved fennel fronds, snipped to short lengths.

Chlodnik

(Polish Beet, Seafood and Meat Soup)

6 portions

- **2 large beets with leaves**
- **salt**
- **1 medium-size cucumber**
- **2 shallots**
- **4 ounces boned cooked veal**
- **12 ounces shrimps**
- **1 tablespoon snipped fresh chives**
- **1 tablespoon minced fresh fennel**
- **1 tablespoon minced fresh dill, or 1 teaspoon dried dillweed**
- **2½ cups chicken stock**
- **1¼ cups light ale**
- **1 tablespoon wine vinegar**
- **1 cup sour cream**
- **1 teaspoon sugar**
- **4 hard-cooked eggs**
- **1 tablespoon chopped fresh parsley**

Cut off the beet greens, wash them, and boil in lightly salted water for 5 minutes. Drain and rinse with cold water. Chop greens and set aside. Scrub the beets and cook in boiling water until tender. Drain, rinse with cold water, and slip off the skins. When cool enough to handle, grate the beets. Set aside. Peel the cucumber and cut into small cubes. Peel and mince the shallots. Cut the veal into small cubes; remove any connective tissue or fat. Poach the shrimps in salted water for 5 minutes, drain, and cool; shell and devein the shrimps.

In a large bowl or soup tureen, combine the cooked beet greens, snipped chives, and minced shallots, fennel and dill. Pour in the chicken stock, ale, vinegar and sour cream. Mix the ingredients thoroughly with a wooden spoon. Purée, if desired.

Stir in 1 teaspoon salt and the sugar and add the shrimps, the cucumber cubes and veal cubes. Place the mixture in the refrigerator for 4 hours.

Just before serving, peel and chop the hard-cooked eggs. Stir the grated beets into the chilled soup. Place a few ice cubes in each of 6 serving bowls and ladle the chilled soup over them. Garnish with chopped egg and the parsley. Serve immediately.

Cream of Cauliflower Soup

4 to 6 portions

- **1 large onion**
- **2 celery ribs**
- **1 medium-size cauliflower**
- **4 tablespoons butter**
- **4 tablespoons flour**
- **1 teaspoon salt**
- **½ teaspoon black pepper**
- **5 cups chicken stock**
- **¼ cup heavy cream**
- **¼ teaspoon grated nutmeg**
- **1 tablespoons minced fresh parsley**

Peel and mince the onion. Wash and dry celery, trim if needed, and mince both ribs and any leaves. Trim cauliflower and separate into flowerets, all about the same size; halve any very large flowerets. Wash and dry any tiny, crisp cauliflower leaves.

Melt the butter in a large heavy saucepan over moderate heat. Add the minced onion and celery and cook, stirring occasionally, for 5 to 7 minutes, until onion is soft and translucent but not browned. Remove pan from heat. With a wooden spoon, stir in the flour, salt and pepper. Gradually pour in the chicken stock, stirring constantly and being careful to avoid lumps. Add the flowerets and the cauliflower leaves. Return pan to heat and bring the soup to a boil, stirring constantly. Reduce heat to low, cover the pan, and simmer for 30 minutes, stirring occasionally.

Remove pan from heat and process the soup in a blender or food processor until reduced to a fine purée. Return the purée to the saucepan and set over low heat. Stir in the cream and cook the soup, stirring constantly, for 5 minutes, until it is hot but not boiling. Remove pan from heat and cool the soup, then chill it.

When ready to serve, check the seasoning, then sprinkle grated nutmeg and chopped parsley over the individual portions.

Plum and Cherry Soup

4 to 6 portions

- **1 pound ripe plums**
- **8 ounces ripe pears**
- **10 ounces stemmed cherries**
- **¼ cup sugar**
- **¼ teaspoon salt**
- **1 teaspoon ground cinnamon**
- **juice and grated rind of 1 lemon**
- **5 cups water**

Wash plums, pears and cherries and halve all of the fruits. Pit plums and cherries, and core the pears. Place the fruits in a large saucepan. Add the sugar, salt, cinnamon and lemon juice and rind. Pour in the water and bring the mixture to a boil over high heat, stirring occasionally. Reduce heat to low, cover the pan, and cook the fruits for 10 to 15 minutes, until tender.

Remove pan from heat. Purée the soup in a food mill, blender or food processor. Return soup to the saucepan. Spoon the cornstarch into a small mixing bowl and stir in 2 tablespoons of the soup. Add the mixture, a little at a time, to the soup, stirring constantly. Set the pan over high heat and bring soup to a boil, stirring. Reduce heat to moderate and cook for 5 to 8 minutes longer, until the soup is smooth and has thickened slightly. Taste the soup and add more sugar if necessary.

Pour the soup into a large serving bowl and set it aside at room temperature to cool. When it is cool, cover the bowl and place it in the refrigerator to chill for 1 hour before serving.

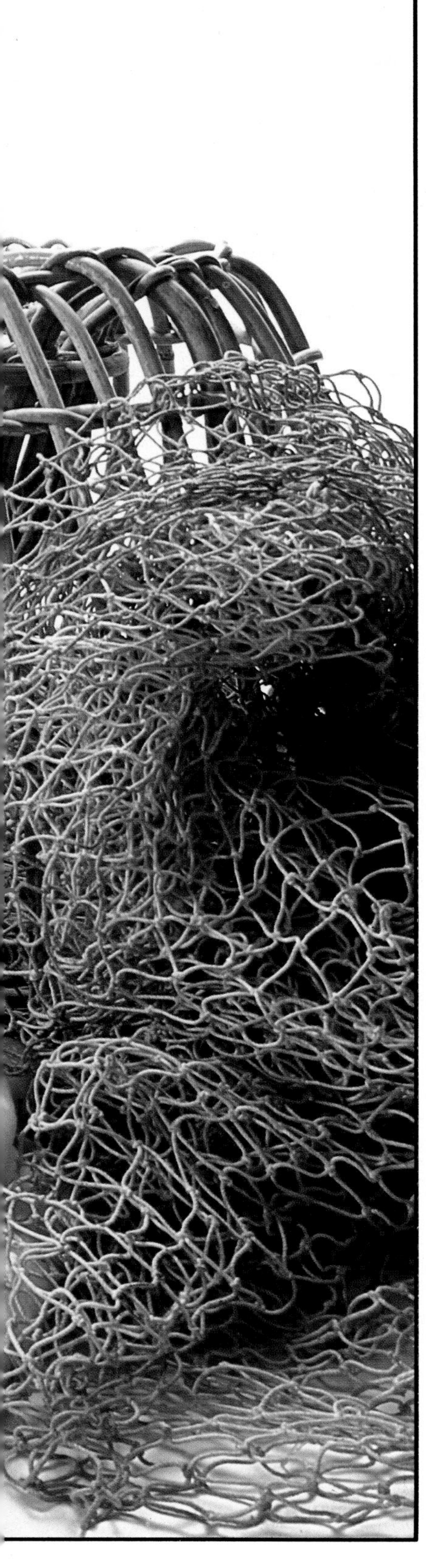

Part Two SHELLFISH

"As for Fish, both Fresh and Salt-Water, of Shell-Fish, and others, no Country can boast of more Variety, greater Plenty, or of better in their several Kinds."

–Robert Beverly, writing about the American Colonies in 1705

Indeed, shellfish were once incredibly abundant on our shores, so much so that according to other contemporary accounts, a person could not walk along the beach without treading on lobsters, clams, oysters, mussels and the like. Early American cookbooks featured many more recipes for shellfish of every sort than we see today. Although shellfish are as popular as ever, the supply is not nearly as ample and accordingly many kinds of shellfish are expensive and considered luxury food.

The shellfish category includes crustaceans—crayfish, crabs, lobsters, shrimps—as well as the mollusks—clams, mussels, oysters, scallops.

Wampum, the strings of beads used as currency among American Indians and their European trading partners, was made from, among other things, the purple hearts of quahog (mahogany clam) shells. The scientific name for the quahog—*Mercenaria mercenaria*—reflects its pecuniary history.

Today clamshells are no longer a source of currency, but the meat contained in them is highly prized and consumed in great quantity. More than 17 million pounds of quahog meat are eaten in the United States every year, appearing fresh on the half-shell, steamed, fried, baked in pies, cut up in chowder and otherwise dealt with in a dozen different ways. Of course, that doesn't include the many other varieties of clams that are less popular, though not necessarily less delicious.

Quahogs are sold in three sizes. The smallest are three to four years old and are called Little Necks after a bay on Long Island, New York. The slightly larger five-year-old clams are called Cherrystones, after Cherrystone Creek, in Virginia. Anything larger than a Cherrystone is known as a chowder clam.

Crab can be considered a truly American dish, since the coastal areas of this continent harbor more edible varieties than any other. The Pacific King and Dungeness crabs, the Atlantic stone and blue crabs, are all shipped widely and are available, fresh or processed, in most parts of the United States.

Softshell crabs, so dear to the hearts of seafood lovers, are nothing more than regular crabs, usually blue crabs, that have recently shed their shells. It is thought that the eating of softshell crabs originated in Louisiana and that the Indians had taught the early settlers how to eat them.

Crayfish, a freshwater cousin of the lobster, which it resembles in shape, inhabit the streams and backwaters of every continent save Africa. Nearly 300 species exist, from the tiny one-inch dwarf crayfish to the great Tasmanian crayfish, which reaches almost eight pounds. Found everywhere in the United States, they are abundant enough for commercial harvesting, primarily in the Pacific Northwest and, of course, Louisiana.

The eating of crayfish has, for centuries, been a seasonal mania among the people of Finland and Sweden as well as among the Cajuns of Louisiana, who spell it crawfish and pronounce it crawfish and eat so much of it that little is left for other parts of the country. Considering the wonderful things that they do with the creatures—everything from crawfish pie, to crawfish gumbo, to crawfish étouffée—who can blame them?

The word "lobster" refers to a number of ten-legged, bottom-dwelling crustaceans, including the spiny lobster, the rock lobster, and their tiny relatives—lobsterettes. Nevertheless, the king of them all, both in terms of size and popularity, is undoubtedly the American lobster *(Homarus americanus)*. Taken primarily in the colder waters off Maine, Nova Scotia and Newfoundland, the adult lobster may range from one to five pounds, though giants of forty pounds or more are not unknown.

Once so plentiful and cheap that they were used for bait, lobsters now bring steep prices, but the delicacy and flavor of the meat make it unlikely that the demand will drop. Lobster has been the basis for many ambitious and justifiably famous recipes such as Lobster Thermidor, Lobster à l'Américaine and Lobster Newburg, but the average American lobster is simply boiled, steamed, or split and broiled, then served up with a dish of lemon butter for a messy, joyous, "hands on" shore dinner.

An Irish folksong celebrates mussel vendors: "They each wheeled their barrow/through streets broad and narrow,/Crying Cockles and mussels! alive, alive oh!" But though they are delicious, plentiful and easily cultivated, mussels are nowhere near as popular in the United States as they are in Europe, where more than 80,000 tons are consumed in France alone. A bivalve mollusk, the mussel grows in large clusters or colonies by attaching itself firmly to rocks by means of extruded fibers called *byssus.* These tough, strong fibers were woven into cloth in ancient Greece, and robes made from this cloth were worn by VIPs on state occasions. But it is these very fibers that may discourage people, first from gathering mussels and subsequently "debearding" them. The blue mussel, named for its typical blue-black color, is by far the most common of the edible species, and many say it is the tastiest. Abundant all along the East Coast, especially in New England, it has also been introduced on the West Coast, where it competes successfully with the indigenous (and also edible, during the cooler months) California mussel.

Despite Dean Swift's much quoted observation that it was a bold man who first ate an oyster, billions of people have followed his example, for oysters are among the oldest of man's staple foods. It has also been among the most popular of foods, both for its delicate taste and texture and for the magical, aphrodisiacal qualities that have been ascribed to it.

Because of the intensity of culinary interest in the oyster, there is a corresponding confusion of names, provenances and conflicting loyalties among oyster fanciers. This results in part from the fact that the taste of an oyster is influenced at least as much by its local environment as by its species. Thus oysters known as Chincoteagues, Blue Points, Cape Cods, or Kent Island are all basically the same animal, *Crassostrea virginica,* while the Belons of France and the Whitstables of England are both *Ostrea edulis.*

Natural oyster beds may be found in bays and river mouths in cold to temperate climates the world over. The oyster thrives in less saline waters where there are fewer of its natural enemies. However, oysters have been cultivated by the Japanese since the seventeenth century, and there are indications that the Romans, who were great lovers of the bivalve, did some systematic transplanting of oysters as much as 2,000 years ago.

The scallop shell is famous as the vehicle of Aphrodite's emergence from the sea and, indeed, its beauty has made it a recurring motif in decorative design and architecture for centuries. It was, as well, the emblem of the apostle Saint James, whose name, translated into French, gives us in turn coquilles Saint-Jacques, the French name for the scallop as well as the well-known variety of creamed scallop dishes.

The preferred species in the United States is the bay scallop, taken primarily up and down the East Coast and around Florida into the Gulf of Mexico. There is also a substantial market for the larger sea scallop. In either case, only the meaty adductor muscle, which holds the two shells together, is consumed in the United States, though the rest of the scallop is considered equally delicious in Europe.

Shrimps are the most valuable part of the American fishery, with about 250 to 300 million pounds landed every year. The seven species caught commercially in this country vary so widely with regard to size, shape and form, that it would take an expert indeed to tell them apart with any assurance. Even less is it possible to tell them apart by their market names, which are at best merely descriptive and at worst deceptive. There is, for instance, virtually no agreement about what may be called a shrimp and what may be called a prawn, although technically the former are marine species and the latter are freshwater.

Because of their unique texture and delicate, distinctive taste, shrimps are among the most versatile of foods. They are featured prominently in such various cuisines as Chinese, French, Japanese, African, Italian, Mexican and American.

SHELLFISH

One of the most popular and versatile foods for cooking is nutritious shellfish. It is rich without being fatty or very caloric. The many varieties are appropriate for all sorts of preparations, from quick family meals to feasts for guests. Numerous forms of shellfish are prized throughout the world; the most commonly available forms in our waters are clams, mussels, oysters, scallops, crabs, shrimps and the most luxurious of all—lobsters.

The flavors of all shellfish share some similarity and the same cooking techniques can be used to prepare them. In many recipes, one shellfish can be substituted for another with ease. Mussels Gratiné, for example, can be made with clams instead of mussels. Mixed Seafood Mayonnaise can be prepared with lump crab meat instead of with lobster. In general, the different mollusks (shellfish with hard outer shells)—clams, mussels, oysters and scallops—and the crustaceans (shellfish with movable, brittle outer shells)—crabs, lobsters and shrimps—substitute well within their own groups. Both kinds can be grouped together to make a mixed shellfish presentation for a spectacular effect. Nothing is as impressive on a buffet as an assembly of clams and oysters on the half-shell and piles of poached shrimps over ice, served simply with lemon wedges and seafood cocktail sauce.

For serving these shellfish at their best, there are two important rules to follow:

Buy them only when absolutely fresh, in many cases still alive.

Cook them for the shortest length of time, so they remain succulent and tender and retain their natural sweet flavor.

Bivalve Mollusks

There may not be a pearl in every oyster, but along with other mollusks oysters form a group of shellfish that provides some of the most delicate and luxurious flavors the sea produces. The family of mollusks includes a wide range of soft-bodied animals, many of them encased in hard protective shells. When the animal is enclosed between two hard shells held together by a strong muscle, it is known as a bivalve mollusk. Clams, mussels, oysters and scallops are all bivalves. Those encased in a single shell, such as conchs, whelks and abalone, are called univalve mollusks.

Although clams, mussels and oysters are found in coastal areas, do not be tempted to gather a free meal from the seashore unless you are sure the area is free from pollution. Check with local fish and game authorities if in doubt; also be sure to have a license in areas where that is required.

Make sure any mollusks you buy are absolutely fresh; clams, mussels and oysters, in the shell, should be alive. Look for tightly closed shells. If shells are open, they should close promptly when given a sharp tap. Buy them from a reputable fish market, which will stock only specimens that are safe to eat, that have been gathered from an approved bed, and that have been well cared for by the fisherman. These days, many fine mussels and oysters are harvested from clean "farmed" beds. They should have a fresh sea aroma; avoid any shellfish with an offensive smell. All edible mollusks decompose rapidly once dead and can become unfit to eat within an hour or two. That is why any clams or mussels that do not open their shells after steaming are discarded. It means they were not alive when they went into the pot. For best results, buy clams, mussels and oysters on the day you plan to eat them, either raw or cooked. Although some may be stored for a few days under refrigeration, every day out of their natural habitat diminishes the flavor and nutritional value.

The shellfish in recipes for clams, mussels, oysters or scallops can easily be interchanged. The quantity of each per dish will be altered to allow for differences in size, but the principles of cooking and the flavoring ingredients remain the same.

These shellfish can be served in soups or sauces, can be sautéed in butter, stuffed in their own shells, baked au gratin or broiled. They also make delicious salads; and they can be used to stuff crêpes, tomatoes and avocados. Use simple cooking methods, since the natural flavor merely needs to be complemented, not improved.

If you are cooking these shellfish in their halved shells, for example with a gratin topping, you will need to support the shells so they do not tip in the baking pan, pouring out their juices. The easiest method is to set the half-shells on a thick layer of rock or coarse (kosher) salt in the bottom of the pan. In a pinch, crumpled aluminum foil can serve to hold the shells steady.

Clams and oysters can also be served raw; see Serving Clams on the Half-Shell and Serving Oysters on the Half-Shell.

Clams

Clams are gathered along both Atlantic and Pacific coasts of the United States and they are a favorite American seafood.

The Atlantic Coast provides the quahog, a hardshell clam, and the soft-shell, as well as the razor clam; the New York area is a main center for the hard-shells. These are sold in a range of sizes: Little Necks are the smallest, Cherrystones are next, and chowder clams are the largest. Chowder clams are used for many recipes in addition to chowder; they can be eaten raw, but are too large to be downed whole, and when very large are somewhat tough.

The Pacific clams include several littlenecks (not related to the eastern Little Neck), butter clams, and other larger species.

Hardshell Clams. Fresh clams are sold alive, in their shells, by the dozen. The shells should be tightly shut

Moules à la Marinière *(Steamed Mussels in Wine Broth)*

Moules à la Marinière (continued)

Mussels are only beginning to achieve their deserved popularity in this country, though Europeans have long appreciated their plump, tender flesh. This method of preparing them—"seaman's wife's style"—is simple and delicious; the mussels are quickly steamed in an aromatic wine broth just until they open. The broth and steamed shellfish are then heaped into soup bowls, to be served with white wine and plenty of crusty bread.

- Count 2 pounds or 1 quart of mussels per person when serving as a first course.
- Be sure the mussels are very well cleaned before cooking. If you need to hold them overnight, sprinkle some flour into the soaking water, which will feed and plump the mussels.
- To sweat vegetables, a technique that draws out their juices into the broth, cook them in butter, covered, over low heat.
- Serve mussels in heated bowls. Soup spoons can be used for the broth, although aficionados of the dish say using a half shell to spoon up the liquor is the best way to savor the flavor to the last drop.
- Provide a large empty bowl for the empty shells.

2 portions

36 mussels
2 or 3 garlic cloves
1 onion
2 shallots or scallions
3 tablespoons butter
1 bouquet garni (see Volume 1, Index)
1 cup dry white wine
1/3 cup water
1 tablespoon chopped parsley

1 Mussels should be absolutely fresh. Tap any open mussels. Discard any that do not shut immediately.

5 When ready to cook, drain the mussels. Mince the garlic, onion and shallots.

6 Melt butter in a large saucepan over low heat. Add vegetables, cover, and sweat for 10 minutes.

10 Reduce the heat and cook for 3 minutes longer to make sure the mussels are cooked.

11 Strain the liquor through cheesecloth into a clean saucepan. Discard any sediment in the pan. Discard bouquet garni.

12 Discard mussels that are still tightly shut. Remove half a shell from each that is open or simply leave both shells attached.

2 Using your hands, pull away beards and any hanging seaweed gripped between the 2 shells.

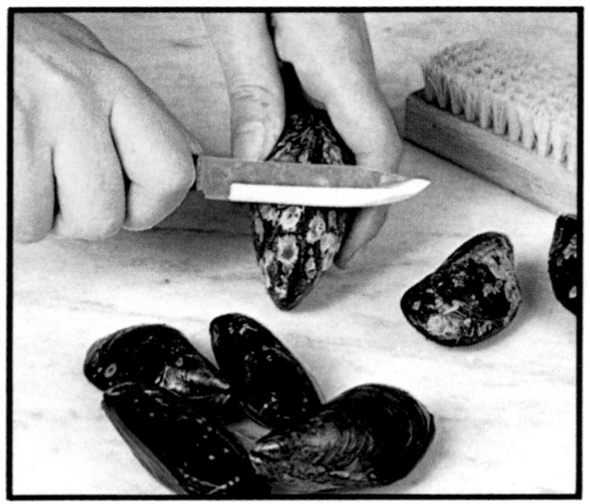

3 Scrub the mussels under cold running water. Scrape away encrustations with a sharp knife.

4 Keep the mussels in a bowl of seawater or salted cold water until ready to cook. Change the water several times.

7 Tie herbs for bouquet garni with a piece of string; or tie them in a square of cheesecloth.

8 Add the bouquet garni, wine and water to the pan. Heat slowly until almost boiling.

9 Add the mussels; cover and cook over high heat, shaking pan occasionally, until shells open. 2 to 4 minutes.

13 Add the mussels on their half shells to the liquor in the pan. Reheat gently.

14 Ladle broth and mussels into serving tureen, heaping up the mussels in the center.

OR Serve in individual bowls. Garnish with parsley.

and there should be no hint of an unpleasant smell around them. Refrigerate them at once after purchasing; they will stay alive under refrigeration for several days.

Fresh clams are also sold shucked, in pint and quart containers; these must be refrigerated immediately and used as soon as possible. Clams are also sold frozen and canned, whole and chopped.

Hardshell clams should be well scrubbed before opening them. For cooked dishes, they can be opened by steaming. To use them raw, they must be cut open with a sharp but blunt-ended clam shucking knife. If you are using a knife, the job will be easier if you put the clams in the freezer for a few minutes; the shells can be pried open more easily when the clams are very cold. Hold the clam with the hinge toward the palm and insert the knife between the shells. Move the knife around to sever the muscle that holds the shells together, open the shells, and then use the knife to release the clam.

Serving Clams on the Half-Shell. Scrub 6 small hardshell clams for each portion, more if you like, or if you are using very small clams such as Little Necks. Use a clam knife to open the clams; do this carefully so as not to lose the clam liquor. Discard the top shells. Free the clams from the bottom shells, but leave clams in them. Rest the shells on a bed of crushed ice. Provide fresh lemon wedges, grated horseradish and Tabasco®. Oyster forks are used to eat the clams (or in more informal settings, they may be raised to your mouth right in the shell). The juices are sipped directly from the shells.

Softshell Clams. These clams take in a large amount of sand, since the shell is never tightly closed. To help them disgorge the sand, immediately place them in a large container of clean seawater, or fresh water with added sea salt; use 1 cup salt to 3 gallons of water. After several hours the clams will get rid of the sand. To test that softshells are alive, touch the neck or siphon; if the clam is alive, it will constrict the neck. Any that do not react are dead; discard them.

Steaming Softshell Clams. Clean the softshells as described, then rinse under cold running water and scrub shells with a stiff brush. Provide 8 to 12 clams for a first course, 12 to 18 for a main dish. Place the clams in a steamer, or in a large pot with a lid. Pour in enough water to reach a depth of 1 inch. Do not add salt. Bring the water rapidly to a boil, then reduce heat until water is just steaming. Cover the pot and steam clams for a few minutes only, just long enough for the shells to open. Stir the clams with wooden spoons to help them cook evenly. Transfer clams to serving bowls. Strain the broth in the pot through a sieve lined with several layers of dampened cheesecloth. For each person, serve ⅓ to ½ cup strained broth in a small bowl and about ¼ cup melted butter in another bowl. Garnish each serving of clams with lemon wedges and make sure there's a peppermill on the table.

Steamed softshells are eaten with the fingers. Remove a clam from its shell, pull off the tough covering of the neck, and dip the clam into the broth to remove any possible grain of sand, then dip into the butter and eat. Lemon juice may be added to the butter, or may be squeezed separately over the clams.

Mussels

The beautiful blue-black shells of the blue or edible mussel can often be seen at low tide around the coast, clinging to rocks or any surface in the intertidal zone. Commercially, mussels are harvested from natural stocks or cultivated mussel beds. These cultivated mussels, which tend to be uniformly sweeter and cleaner, are sold packaged and dated in many supermarkets across the United States. Mussels are also sold frozen, canned, bottled in brine and smoked. The mussel recipes here are all designed for fresh mussels.

Although mussels take time to clean and prepare, the cooking time is brief. Once cooked, they should be eaten as soon as possible, because if kept hot they dry out, lose their flavor, and become tough. Although, like clams, mussels can be opened with a knife, they more often are steamed open. Once opened, they can be served either hot or cold. A steaming bowl of Moules à la Marinière and piquant Mussel and Potato Salad are both colorful dishes. Mussels are also delicious stuffed and gratinéed, served in a creamy sauce, or wrapped in crisp bacon. Because they are low in fat, mussels combine well with sauces enriched with egg yolks or cream, with mayonnaise, buttered bread crumbs and bacon. Curry powder and aniseed both enhance the flavor of mussels.

Mussels are at their best from September through March. In late spring and summer months they spawn, and both taste and texture are inferior. When buying them in the shell, check that the shells are shut, or that they close tightly when tapped. Any that are not shut or do not close can be presumed to be dead and should be discarded, as they deteriorate rapidly after death.

Fresh mussels are usually sold by weight. A pound in shells will give you 3 to 4 ounces of shelled meat. If you are serving them in the shell, as for Moules à la Marinière, allow 18 to 24 mussels per person. It is impossible to judge the size of the mussel from the size of the shell, so be sure to purchase a few extra for each portion.

Preparing Mussels. Mussels need careful cleaning to rid them of sand and dirt on the shells, and the beards, threadlike strands that were used by the shellfish to anchor it to a post or rock, must be cut away. Treat mussels like softshell clams: tip them into a large container and cover them with seawater or salted freshwater. Remove mussels one at a time and scrub the shells with a wire brush to get rid of mud, sand and grit. Pull the plantlike dark beard from each one, trimming any stubborn ones with a sharp knife. Discard any that have floated to the top of the water, any that are cracked or broken, any that are gaping open and do not close when tapped, and any very heavy shells, which are probably mudders, full of mud and sand.

When the mussels are cleaned and sorted, place them in a container of fresh seawater or salted freshwater and leave for an hour or two to disgorge any sand. When you are ready to cook, give mussels a final rinse in cold water.

Steam mussels open with only a small amount of liquid and added flavorings. As they steam, they will release quite a lot of liquid of their own. The heat required to steam them open is sufficient to cook them lightly. If they are to be added to a sauce, soup, pie or batter later, they will need only reheating in the final dish, not recooking. Prolonged cooking or reheating, or even keeping them hot, will dry out and toughen the mussels. If you have several layers in the steamer, turn them with wooden spoons halfway through the steaming time to make them cook more evenly; or close the pot tightly and shake it to move the mussels around.

Steaming the mussels with liquid and flavorings provides mussel liquor, which can make a delicious addition to a sauce. It is essential to strain this liquor. Pour it through a fine-mesh sieve lined with several layers of dampened cheesecloth; strain it a second time if the mussels were very sandy to begin with. However carefully you have washed the shells, some grit always lingers and this would be unpleasant in a soup or sauce. Discard any mussels that have not opened. For some recipes they should remain in both shells, for others they are placed on the half-shell, and for salads they are removed from the shells completely.

Oysters

Believe it or not, oysters used to be a poor man's food. They were available in abundance and were an excellent source of protein in an otherwise unsatisfactory diet. Unfortunately this is no longer true. Oyster beds were ruthlessly exploited in an endeavor to keep up with the demand, and pollution damaged many natural areas. Now only careful cultivation has preserved this pearl of the sea.

Oysters are available fresh in the shell, shucked in containers, frozen, canned, packed in brine, and smoked. They are graded for sale in sizes small, medium or large. (In Europe there is numerical grading by weight.) The grade refers to the size before opening, and not to the quality. Good oysters are plump, but it does not necessarily follow that large shells produce the best oysters. Be guided by the advice of a reputable fish market. Oysters are at their best in the cool months.

If opening oysters at home is daunting, ask your market to open them for you and to pack them on ice, on the half-shell. Request a separate container of the oyster liquor in case any spills.

Oysters are often sold by the dozen, which was traditionally 1 portion when served raw. Today we are more likely to serve half that many for a first course. In cooked main dishes allow 8 to 12 oysters per portion.

Serving Oysters on the Half-Shell. Oysters do not need to be cleaned in any way. They just need to be opened. To open firmly closed oysters, you need a short-bladed, blunt, sturdy knife. If you plan to have oysters often, it is worth investing in a proper oyster knife. Freshly opened oysters have an exhilarating flavor that soon begins to evaporate; the surrounding liquor is an essential part of their goodness, and they must be opened carefully to retain the liquor.

Opening Oysters

1 **Wrap one hand in a clean cloth and hold the oyster in your palm. The curved shell should be downward and the hinge toward you.**

2 **Insert a knife between the shells near the hinge to sever the muscle. Grip with your fingers and twist the knife to force the shells apart.**

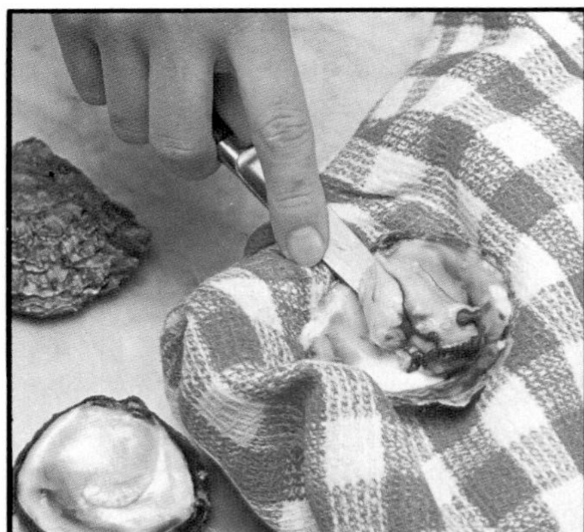

3 **Lift off the flat shell and slip the knife under the oyster to free it from the deep shell. Remove any chips of shell.**

Removing Crab Meat from the Shell

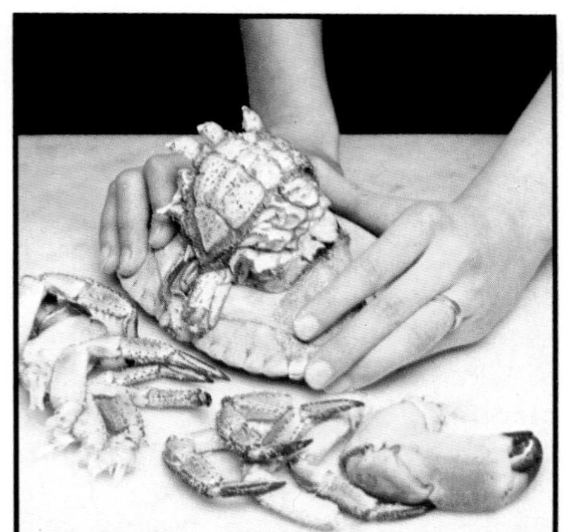

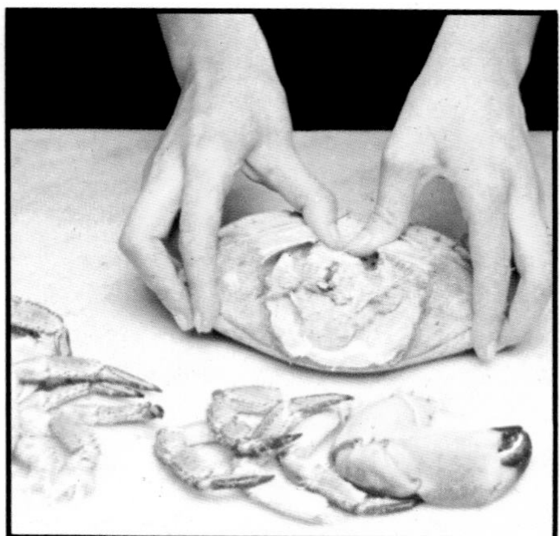

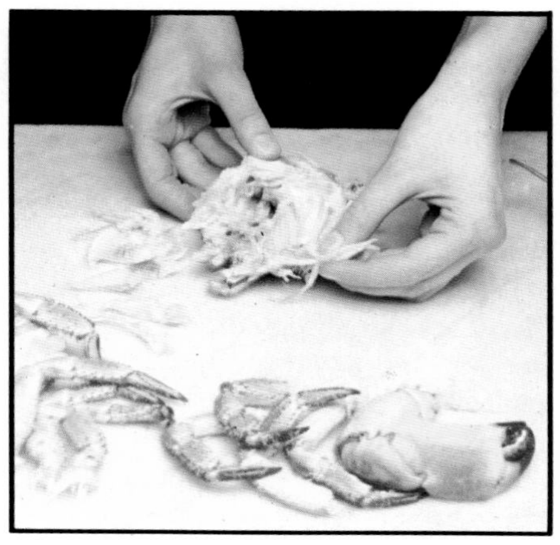

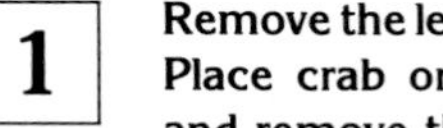

Remove the legs and large claws. Place crab on its back. Lift up and remove the apron.

2 **With hands, carefully remove and discard the stomach sac and any spongy matter from the shell.**

3 **Pull off and discard the feathery gills. Scoop out the meat from the claws and any from the legs.**

Begin the operation by wrapping the hand in which you will hold the oyster, to protect the hand from the rough shells and any nicks from the knife. The job is messy, as liquor tends to spill out. Hold oyster firmly in the palm of the wrapped hand, curved shell downward and the hinge toward you. Press the oyster knife between the shells, near the hinge, and slide it around until you sever the muscle that holds the shells together. Hold the oyster firmly with the wrapped hand and with the other hand jerk the knife upward to pry the shells apart. Continue to free the oyster from the top shell, and lift off that shell. Slip the knife under the oyster to free it from the curved shell. Flick off any chips of shell.

Reserve as much of the liquor as possible. You may not be very successful in your first few attempts, so buy a few extra oysters for practice. When the oysters have been opened, put them at once on the serving plate so that the liquor will not be spilled accidentally. Unless you have oyster dishes, arrange the curved oyster shells on a bed of finely crushed ice. Embed them in the ice to hold them steady, with the hinges toward the center. Place a large lemon wedge on the end of an oyster fork in the center of the dish. A few drops of lemon juice can be squeezed over each oyster before eating. Some people also like seafood cocktail sauce, a few drops of Tabasco®, or a dab of horseradish. Another good sauce is mignonnette, a blending of shallots, vinegar and black pepper. Use the fork to eat the oyster, then pick up the shell in your fingers and drink the liquor. Serve with thin slices of brown bread and butter or oyster crackers and a chilled dry white wine. Chablis is the classic accompaniment.

Oysters may be served in a mixed seafood hors d'oeuvre. Arrange them in the same way but add clams on the half-shell, and some cooked mussels and shrimps.

Cooking Oysters. Although most oyster lovers agree that the finest way to eat them is raw, there are people who prefer them cooked. Do not overcook them or they will toughen. They must be simmered gently just until the edges ruffle slightly but do not actually curl. The exact time will depend on the type and size of the oyster.

If you are cooking oysters in the shell, embed the half-shells in a pan of rock or coarse (kosher) salt to steady the shells so they retain the oyster juices and whatever other ingredient the recipe requires.

Oysters are also used in soup, gumbo, sauced dishes, skewered dishes in combination with chicken livers or bacon, fritters, pies made with chicken or turkey, and they are delicious scalloped.

Scallops

Scallops are among the most delicate and delicious of shellfish. Both tiny bay scallops and the larger sea scallops are succulent, with good flavor. Scallops are sold fresh, by weight, and frozen.

In European coastal areas scallops are sold in the shell, so one has the whole shellfish, and all of it is edible in the same way as an oyster is. Since the scallop does not keep its shells tightly closed like a clam or oyster, it begins to dry out as soon as removed from the sea. Therefore, away from the coast, scallops are opened and only the adductor muscle is retained. In European markets the coral, looking like an orange tongue, is retained as well, but in American markets we get only the white muscle.

In areas such as Nantucket Bay the little bay scallops are fished from November to April. The adductor muscle is very small, about ½ inch thick, and is considerably more tender and

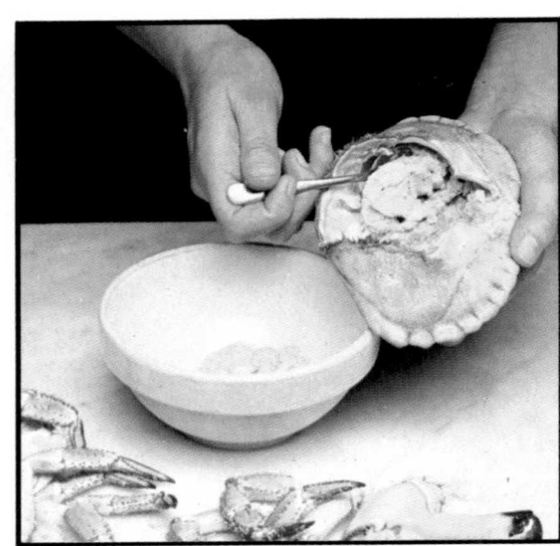

4 Using a skewer or 2-pronged fork, scoop out the flesh from the shell. Add it to the claw meat.

sweeter in flavor than the sea scallop muscle. In October in the Nantucket area family scalloping allows the lucky residents to have the whole scallop, or just the muscle and the coral. The small scallops are also fished all along the Atlantic Coast as far as the Gulf of Mexico.

Many so-called fresh scallops are actually recently defrosted. They will be safe to eat and taste good, but they will not be as delicious as scallops that have not been frozen. Scallops are often soaked by the distributors, another process that diminishes the flavor.

Preparing Scallops. Scallops need little preparation. Cut off the small piece of gristle attached to the muscle, as this toughens in cooking. Put the scallops in a sieve and dip this quickly into a bowl of room-temperature water. Drain well, then quickly pat them dry in paper towels or a clean cloth. Do not soak scallops. If you are using frozen scallops, defrost them and roll in a towel to dry in the same way.

To preserve the delicate flavor as well as the succulence, do not overcook scallops, which dries the flesh, or smother them with strong additional flavors. The simplest ways of cooking are the best.

Scallops must be cooked just before serving. Do not plan to cook in advance as they will lose moisture and flavor if kept waiting. Scallops are delicious sautéed, broiled, deep fried, briefly poached, baked in shells, or served in soups, sauces and salads.

The French name *coquille Saint-Jacques* (St. James shell) is often used for various scallop dishes, and the shell itself can serve as a container for baking and serving.

Crustaceans

These shellfish have jointed bodies covered with an external skeleton, two pairs of antennae, and according to the species legs or swimmerets or both. Some have large front claws. This group includes all the various kinds of crabs, lobsters, lobsterettes, and shrimps, as well as crayfish, prawns and barnacles, all of which are edible. There are no recipes here for crayfish or barnacles, since they are not often commercially available on the retail level. As for prawns and lobsterettes, they can be prepared in the same ways as shrimps; if you find frozen lobsterettes in your market under the mysterious names of Danish lobster tails or Dublin Bay prawns, don't hesitate to purchase and enjoy them.

Crab

The most common crab in eastern North America is the blue crab, abundant in the Gulf of Mexico and Chesapeake Bay. This crab has the last pair of legs flattened for swimming. Like other crabs, it has two large claws. These crabs are sold live, usually packed in seaweed; in some markets cooked crabs in the shell may be available. The crab meat is sold fresh, frozen and canned.

It is these crabs that become softshells, at the time when they shed their shells in the process of growth. Because the new shells start to become hard almost at once, the crabs are gathered just before shedding, so they can be sold when perfectly tender and plump. Softshells are in season in late spring and early summer. They are eaten whole, claws, shells and all, usually sautéed or deep-fried.

Blue crabs come inshore in warm weather. The meat is rich in phosphorus. The female crabs carry eggs, which are used in some special recipes such as South Carolina she-crab soup.

Spider crabs are so called because of the way the legs grow around their somewhat pear-shaped bodies, rather like a spider's legs. The name is used for several different species, all of them quite large. Meat from these crabs is usually marketed as snow crab or queen crab.

Because of their size Alaskan King crabs are rarely sold whole, but are usually processed on the fishing vessel. The legs, in shells, are sold frozen, and the shelled meat is sold frozen or defrosted.

Other crabs that come to American markets include the large Dungeness on the West Coast, and the red crab—red before cooking—which is similar to the King crab. The stone crab, found in southern waters, provides claws, which are sold cooked in the shell, or sometimes frozen after cooking.

Buying Crab. Fresh crab meat is often sold in dated containers. It is highly perishable and should be eaten as soon as possible. It will keep overnight in the refrigerator, but not much longer.

Freshness is the most important consideration when buying cooked crabs in the shell. Appearance and smell will help you to determine the degree of freshness. The crab should not look dried up, and it should feel heavy for its size. If you shake a boiled crab, it should not sound as if there is a lot of liquid inside. A good fishmonger will not sell crabs that are hollow and contain a lot of water.

Live crabs should be lively, with all the claws intact.

Canned crab meat is readily available and is good to have on hand for emergencies. It may be labeled lump, flake or claw meat. Lump meat is large pieces from the body and flake meat is smaller bits from the body. The best

Removing the Meat from a Cooked Lobster

1 Wipe the lobster with a clean damp cloth. Twist off the claws and all the legs; set aside.

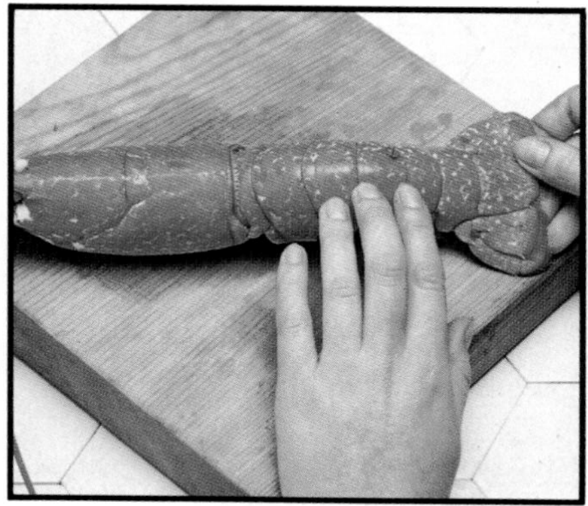

2 Place body, back uppermost, on a chopping board, with head on the left and tail extended.

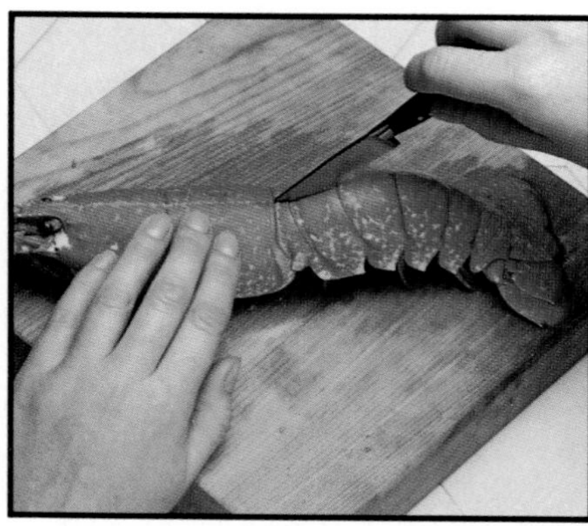

3 Insert a pointed knife in the center of the back just below the junction of the head and the body.

6 Remove and discard the intestinal tract, which runs the length of the body, and the sand sac in the head.

7 Remove and reserve the coral (roe) and the green tomalley (liver) if there is any.

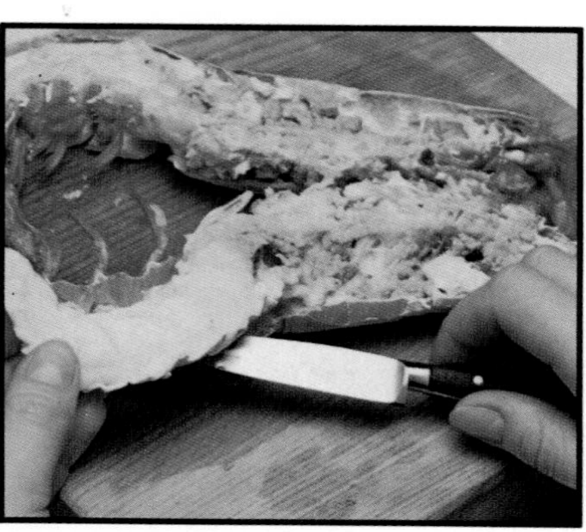

8 The meat can be left in the shell or can be removed and cut up to be served in a sauce.

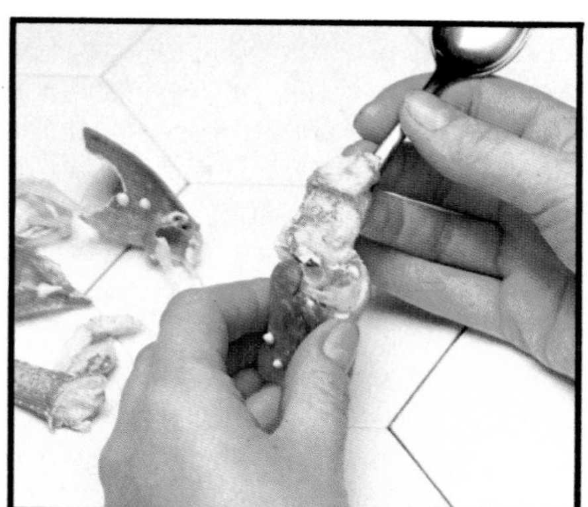

11 Remove meat from the smaller joints of the claws with the handle of a teaspoon or a lobster pick.

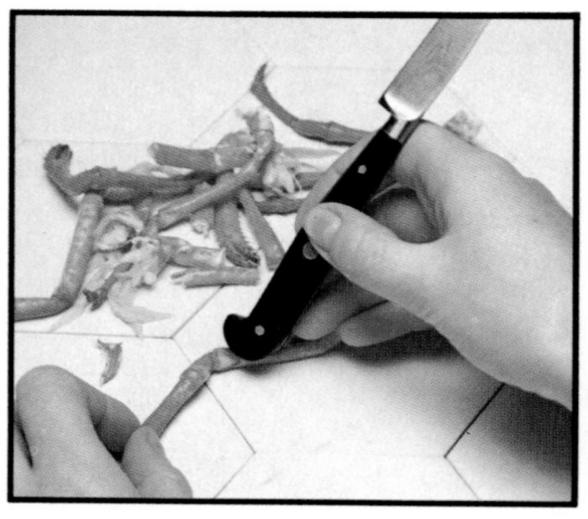

12 Crack the legs with the handle of a knife and pull out the meat.

OR For neat tail slices, cut lobster through the shell where the carapace joins the tail.

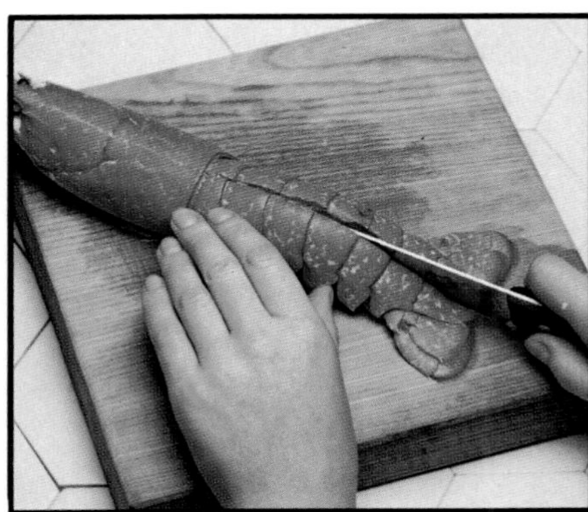

4 Halve the lobster by cutting lengthwise along the center of the back to the tail.

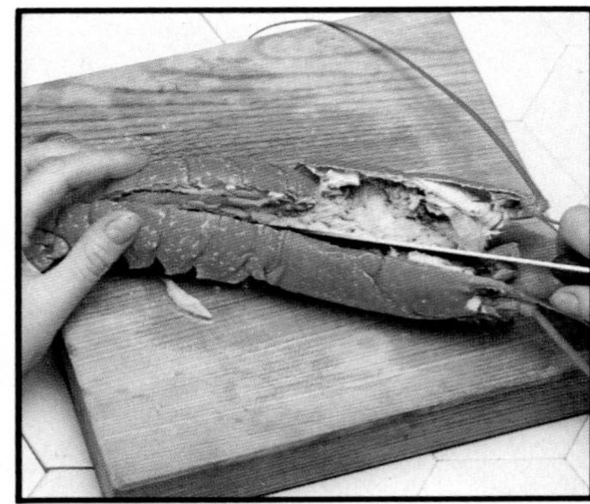

5 Turn lobster around and cut through the middle of the head until lobster is entirely halved.

9 Tap around the broadest part of each claw until the shell cracks and can be pulled apart.

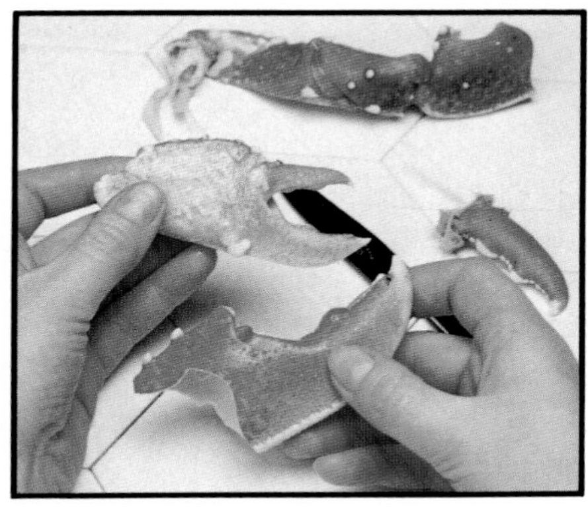

10 Sever the cartilage between small pincer and main claw and pull out the meat in one piece.

ε Cut away the soft undershell of the tail with scissors. Lift out the meat in one piece.

ε Cut the tail meat into thin slanting slices, called medallions.

canned crab is pasteurized and referred to as "fresh-canned." You can find it at your fishmonger's if not in your supermarket. Frozen crab meat from blue crabs is sold, as well as that from spider and King crabs and the stone crab claws.

If you wish to prepare your own crab meat for storage, after boiling and shelling it can be frozen and stored for up to 1 month, although fresh tastes more delicate and has a better texture.

For 4 portions for a main course, purchase 2 to 3 pounds of crabs in shells. Usually, half of the total weight is in the shells, so allow for this when calculating the amount you need. Two pounds of crabs will yield approximately 1 pound of edible meat (but it can be much less).

If you are serving softshells or any crab in the shell, allow 3 to 4 crabs per person, depending on size. Sometimes softshells are very tiny; in that case, prepare more.

Cooking Live Crabs. If you are preparing your own crabs, you will need a wooden board on which to work, a teaspoon for scraping meat from the shell, a small and a heavy knife, a 1-pound weight or a clean hammer to crack the claws, a skewer or nut pick to help dig out the meat from the legs, bowls to collect the meat, and a large piece of newspaper to collect all the shells and debris.

First hold the crab across the back under cold running water to wash off any dirt and scraps of seaweed. Drop the crabs head first into a large kettle of boiling water. Once the water returns to the boil, simmer the crabs for 15 to 20 minutes, depending on size, until all the shells turn red. Do not overcook crab or the meat will become watery and lose flavor.

Crabs can be cooked in court bouillon or in water flavored with crab boil (available where spices are sold), or they can be steamed. When crabs are done, lift them out with tongs and rinse with cold water.

Crabs can be split with a cleaver and cleaned before cooking if you prefer, but it is easier to clean them after cooking.

Lobster Thermidor

2 portions

- 1 lobster, 2 pounds, freshly boiled
- 1 shallot, peeled and minced
- ¼ cup dry white wine or dry vermouth
- 2 tablespoons butter
- 3 tablespoons brandy
- ½ cup Béchamel Sauce (see Volume 3 Index)
- 2 tablespoons heavy cream or crème fraîche
- ½ teaspoon prepared Dijon-style mustard
- pinch of cayenne pepper
- salt and white pepper
- 2 tablespoons grated Parmesan or Gruyère cheese
- parsley sprigs, for garnish

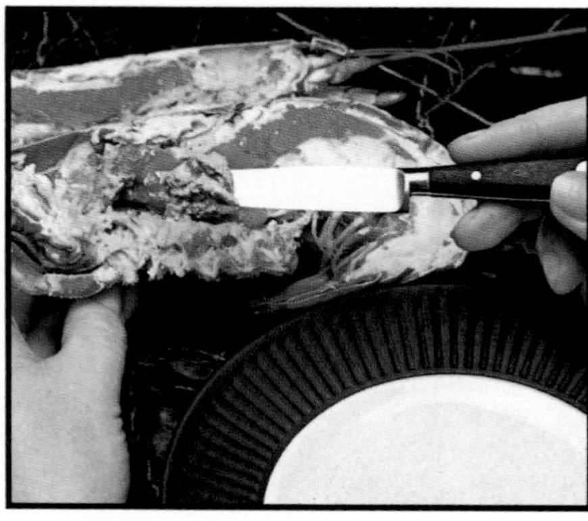

1 Prepare lobster by splitting lengthwise. Remove the coral and green tomalley and reserve both.

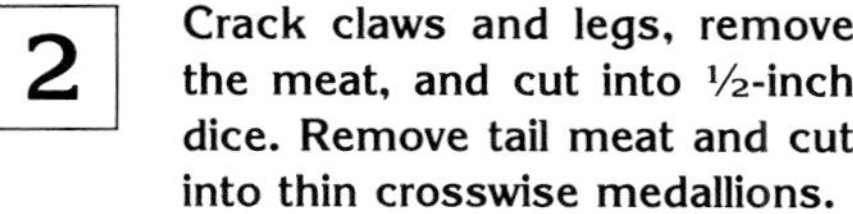

2 Crack claws and legs, remove the meat, and cut into ½-inch dice. Remove tail meat and cut into thin crosswise medallions.

3 In a small saucepan, simmer shallot with wine or vermouth until wine is reduced by half.

4 Melt 1 tablespoon of the butter in a large skillet. Add lobster meat and cook over moderate heat until just heated through; shake pan occasionally.

5 Measure the brandy into a metal ladle. Warm over flame, ignite it and pour over lobster. Shake the pan until flames subside.

6 Add béchamel sauce and cream to wine reduction and bring to a boil. Stir in mustard, cayenne, and salt and pepper to taste.

7 Reduce heat, sieve coral and tomalley, stir into sauce, and pour the sauce over the lobster, stirring gently to mix.

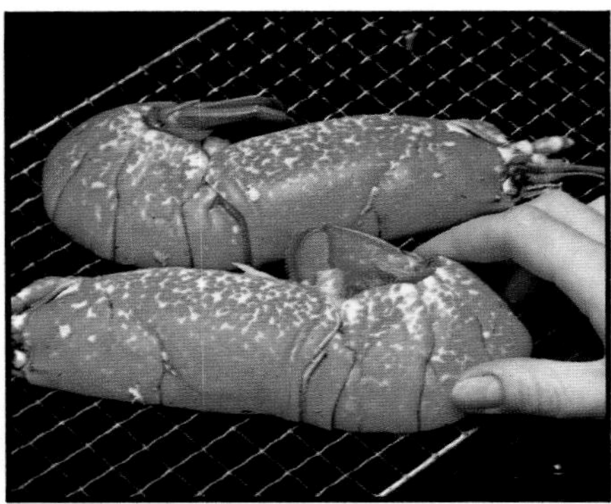

8 Preheat broiler. Place empty shells, cut sides down, under broiler to heat and dry them.

9 Remove dry shells and fill them with lobster mixture. Sprinkle cheese on top and dot with remaining butter.

10 Broil about 4 inches from heat source for 2 to 4 minutes, until hot, golden and bubbling. Serve garnished with parsley.

A more humane way to proceed is to kill the crab before boiling it. Drive a pointed knife or a skewer into the brain, which is on the underside of the body near the eyes. Then drop the crab into boiling water.

Removing Cooked Crab from the Shell. Taking the meat from the shell is known as "dressing" the crab. When the cooked crab is cool, lay it on its back with the tail flap toward you. Twist off the legs and claws as close as possible to the body. Lift up and remove the apron, then insert the fingers between shell and body and force them apart. Or pry the two sections apart with the tip of a knife.

Start with the body section. First remove and discard the gills (known as dead man's fingers). These grayish-white frondlike pieces are inedible. Remove and discard the stomach sac, which lies just below the head. Any green matter in the shell should be discarded. Carefully scrape out the meat from the shell, using the handle of a teaspoon to get under the edge of the shell. Dig the meat out of the holes left by the legs and claws with a skewer or nut pick. Wrap the claws in a kitchen towel and crack them with a weight or a hammer. Remove the meat, taking care not to include any shell splinters. Crack the legs to extract the small amount of meat in them, or leave them intact for garnishing.

Lobster

The flesh of even large lobsters is delicate and delicious. It has a nutty, sweet flavor and a succulent, tender, yet firm texture.

To taste lobster at its best, eat it soon after cooking, either hot or just cold. Fancy sauces and garnishes are superfluous, as they mask rather than enhance the lobster's natural flavor. However, glamorous dishes devised by eminent chefs make spectacular use of this crustacean. It can be served as the classical Lobster Thermidor (see Index) or in a delicious sauce, such as Newburg or Mornay.

Demand for lobster far exceeds the supply, which makes it expensive. This means it is usually reserved for special occasions. All the more reason to know how to cook a lobster to make the most of its unique quality.

American lobsters are blue-black in color when alive, but turn bright red when cooked. They have a smooth shell and are easily identified by their two large claws of unequal size, which terminate in movable pincers.

Rock lobster or spiny lobster, also called crawfish, *langouste* in French, is similar in size to an American lobster, but is easily distinguished by its tiny claws, rough spiny shell and long antennae. They do not have the large front claws. They are reddish brown when alive and turn brick red when cooked. The texture and flavor is similar to that of the American lobster, though not as delicate, especially when frozen. It is the tails of this lobster that are sold as lobster tails, available in supermarkets the year around.

Lobsterettes, in French *langoustines,* in Italian *scampi,* are a separate species, distributed all over the world. Their shape and the large front claws, like a large lobster, show that they are members of the lobster family and not some kind of shrimp.

Buying Lobster. Lobsters are usually purchased alive and whole. Look for lobsters that are lively and have both claws intact. Some people ask for a female because of the delicious coral (roe). If the lobster is cooked, choose it carefully. It should feel heavy for its size, and have a bright red, crisp, dry shell, a pleasant sweet smell and a springy tail. Avoid cooked lobsters with loose, slack joints.

Lobsters are graded according to size: chicken, about 1 pound; quarters, 1 to 1½ pounds; large, 1½ to 2½ pounds; jumbo, anything over 2½ pounds. Large lobsters are usually cheaper per pound and a good buy for salads and sauced dishes, as the meat yield is better.

A male lobster has heavier claws than a female, the center fin of the tail is narrow, and the first pair of swimmerets beneath the tail are horny rather than soft. When in roe the female lobster provides eggs in the form of red coral (immature roe) found in the carapace. Lobsters reproduce only every two years and the female carries her eggs for nearly a year, so coral is common at all seasons. The immature roe has a better flavor and color than the extruded roe, which is found beneath the tail. Lobster roe can be pounded to add color and flavor to sauces and butters. You can recognize a female lobster by the broadness of the tail and the fact that all the swimmerets are soft.

Lobster is also sold canned and frozen, and the meat is sold fresh in some markets in coastal areas.

Purchase a 1- to 1½-pound lobster for each portion if you are buying them live. If you are buying the shelled meat, fresh, frozen or canned, allow 4 to 8 ounces per portion.

Cutting up Live Lobster. For recipes in which the lobster is cooked in pieces, still in the shell, the lobster needs to be cut up. Kill the lobster by laying it on its back and plunging the point of a sharp knife crosswise into its body just below the spot at which the head and chest join. Or, if you prefer, plunge the lobster head first into a kettle of rapidly boiling water, cover, and boil for 1 minute.

Lay the lobster, belly down on a chopping board. Place the blade of a stout kitchen knife at the point where the carapace meets the tail, and hit the knife with a mallet or other weight to separate the tail. Cut off the claws where they join the body and crack the claw shells. Cut the tail across in slices following the joints. Split the head lengthwise; discard the stomach sac and the intestinal tract. Take out the coral if there is any and the green tomalley (the liver), and set them aside for adding to the sauce.

One way to cook a fresh lobster is to sauté these pieces still in shells, in butter or oil, and to serve it in a sauce that incorporates the lobster juices. The lobster is cooked through when the shell turns red and the meat is firm and opaque, about 10 minutes. However, the best way to serve lobster is simply either boiled or broiled.

Peeling Cooked Shrimps

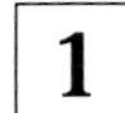

1 If the shrimps have heads on, leave for garnish. Or, if you prefer, just twist to separate.

2 Save the heads and shells for making fish stock, soups or sauces.

3 Cut down the back of the shrimp with a small sharp knife and remove the black vein.

Shrimps

Shrimps are our most popular shellfish. They are found all over the world. The size ranges from 2 to a pound to 180 to a pound, and all sizes are fished and sold. Shrimps are also being farmed in various parts of the world.

Shrimps are marketed fresh; frozen, both cooked and raw; canned; smoked; dried; and as shrimp paste. Usually shrimps are sold without their heads; if you purchase some that still retain their heads, they may be cooked that way, or the heads can easily be snapped off.

Shrimp sizes at market are small, over 40 to the pound; medium, 31 to 40 per pound; large, 21 to 30 per pound; extra large, 16 to 20 per pound; jumbo, up to 15 per pound.

Shrimps can be found in supermarkets as well as in fish markets. Loose shrimps sold in fish markets as fresh may have been frozen at one time. Flash-frozen shrimps, peeled and deveined, are excellent. If the shrimps you buy are already cooked, be sure to reduce cooking time for any dish in which you use them.

Cooking Shrimps. Shrimps are quick to cook; the flavor can easily be ruined by overcooking, and the texture as well. Bring a pan of salted water to a boil. Put in the shrimps and bring back to the boil. By the time the water boils, the shrimps will probably be cooked, or will need only another ½ to 1 minute. (Larger specimens will need another 2 to 3 minutes.) Test one to see if it is cooked. If it is underdone it will be soggy; if overdone it will be hard. Perfectly cooked shrimps are loosely curled.

Alternatively, put shrimps in a tightly covered pan and set over high heat to cook in their own juices. Shake the pan occasionally and cook for about 10 minutes. Or cover them with water and bring to a boil; at once pour off the water and leave shrimps in the pot, covered, to cook in the steam remaining.

Shrimps may be cooked in their shells, then shelled and deveined; or they may be shelled and deveined before cooking. They may be served in the shell or not, but for most purposes it is better to shell them before serving. If your guests are peeling their own shrimps, be sure to provide them with plates for the shells, finger bowls and extra napkins.

Shrimps may be deveined without removing the shells; simply split the shell down the back and use a small knife to lift out the intestinal tract. Shrimps may be butterflied for certain recipes. Split them almost through, leaving the tail feathers or the last tail segment in place to hold the shrimp together.

Serving Cooked Shrimps. Freshly cooked shrimps can be served immediately, which shows off their salty, yet sweet, taste to best advantage. Or they can be mixed into sauces while still warm—clarified butter and lemon wedges, hollandaise, tomato-based sauces. Or they can be chilled and served in salads, with mayonnaise or vinaigrette, or simply with lemon wedges.

Large shrimps, which have been only barely cooked, can be placed on an oiled rack, brushed with herb-flavored oils or herb butter, and finished off under the broiler.

Serve freshly cooked shrimps on a bed of crushed ice, with a bowl of hard-cooked eggs, some radishes or tomatoes, watercress and lettuce hearts. Accompany with fresh brown bread and butter, a bowl of coarse salt, a dressing of olive oil, lemon juice and minced fresh herbs.

Mussel and Potato Salad

4 portions

- **3 pounds mussels**
- **1½ pounds boiling potatoes**
- **8 tablespoons olive oil**
- **¾ cup dry white wine**
- **2 garlic cloves**
- **¼ cup chopped parsley**
- **2 celery ribs**
- **2 medium-size tomatoes**
- **2 tablespoons white-wine vinegar**
- **½ teaspoon prepared Dijon-style mustard**
- **salt and black pepper**

Scrub and debeard the mussels. Scrub the potatoes. Cook the potatoes in a large saucepan of boiling water until tender, 25 to 35 minutes. Meanwhile, in another large saucepan heat 2 tablespoons of the oil over high heat. Add the mussels, cover tightly, and cook, shaking the pan frequently, until the mussels open, 5 to 7 minutes. Remove mussels from the pan and discard any that have not opened. Pour the mussel cooking liquid through a fine-mesh sieve lined with several layers of dampened cheesecloth. Pour the strained liquid into a medium-size nonaluminum saucepan and add the wine. Peel garlic and put through a press into the liquid. Add 2 tablespoons of the parsley and boil the mixture over high heat until reduced to ½ cup.

When the potatoes are cooked, drain them. As soon as they are cool enough to handle, peel and slice them. Put the warm sliced potatoes into a serving bowl, pour the hot reduced liquid over them, and toss. Let stand until cool, tossing occasionally.

Wash and dry the celery and chop it. Wash and core tomatoes and cut into wedges. Remove mussels from their shells, reserving a few in the shell for garnish. Add the mussels and chopped celery to the cooled potatoes; toss lightly to mix. In a small bowl, whisk together the vinegar and mustard. Gradually whisk in remaining 6 tablespoons olive oil to make a vinaigrette. Season with salt and pepper to taste. Pour the vinaigrette over the salad and toss gently until potatoes and mussels are coated. Sprinkle remaining parsley on top. Garnish the salad with tomato wedges and the reserved mussels in the shell.

Linguine with Mussels and Clams

4 portions

- **2 pounds mussels**
- **2 dozen Little Neck clams**
- **1 medium-size onion**
- **2 shallots**
- **3 garlic cloves**
- **1½ pounds ripe tomatoes, or 3½ cups canned peeled plum tomatoes**
- **5 tablespoons olive oil**
- **½ cup dry white wine**
- **3 parsley sprigs**
- **½ bay leaf**
- **salt and freshly ground black pepper**
- **1 pound uncooked linguine, or other long thin pasta**
- **2 tablespoons chopped fresh parsley**

Scrub and debeard the mussels, and scrub the clams. Peel and mince the onion. Peel and chop the shallots. Peel garlic cloves and put through a press. Blanch, peel and seed the tomatoes, and chop them; if using canned tomatoes, drain, seed and chop them; remove as many seeds as possible from the tomatoes.

Heat 3 tablespoons of the oil in a large nonaluminum skillet or flameproof casserole over moderate heat. Add the onion and cook, stirring frequently, until softened but not browned, about 3 minutes. Add the garlic and cook for about 30 seconds, until fragrant. Stir in the tomatoes, reduce heat, and simmer gently, uncovered, until tomatoes are reduced to a purée and excess liquid has evaporated, 15 to 20 minutes. Remove from heat and set aside.

Pour the wine into a large nonaluminum saucepan and add the shallots, parsley sprigs and bay leaf. Bring to a boil over high heat. Add the mussels, cover and cook, shaking the pan frequently, for 5 to 7 minutes, until the mussels just open. Remove mussels from the saucepan and discard any that are not opened. Reserve some of the mussels on their half-shells for garnish; remove the rest from their shells and set aside. Strain the cooking liquid through a fine-mesh sieve lined with several layers of dampened cheesecloth; reserve the strained mussel liquid.

Pour ¼ cup water into a large saucepan and bring to a boil over high heat. Add the clams and steam them, shaking the pan, for 5 to 7 minutes, until clams just open. Remove them from the saucepan, and discard any that are not opened. Reserve some on their half-shells for garnish; remove the rest from their shells and add to the mussels. Strain the cooking liquid through a fine-mesh sieve lined with several layers of dampened cheesecloth. Pour the strained clam and mussel liquids into a clean saucepan. Boil over moderately high heat until reduced to ⅔ cup.

Meanwhile, bring 6 quarts of water to a boil for the pasta. Add the reduced shellfish liquid to the tomato purée. Bring to a simmer and cook, stirring, until the mixture is reduced to a thick sauce consistency. Season with salt and pepper to taste. Add 2 tablespoons salt to the pot of water and drop in the linguine. Cook for 8 to 10 minutes, until *al dente,* tender but still resistant to the bite. Drain pasta and toss with remaining 2 tablespoons olive oil in a large shallow bowl.

Quickly add the shelled mussels and clams to the sauce and heat them for about 1 minute. Pour the sauce over the pasta and toss lightly to mix. Arrange the reserved mussels and clams on the half-shell around the edge of the bowl. Sprinkle parsley over the top and serve immediately.

Note: This dish from the Bay of Naples is traditionally served without grated cheese.

Sautéed Scallops

6 portions

- **1½ pounds bay scallops or sea scallops**
- **12 triangles of white bread, toasted**
- **4 tablespoons unsalted butter**
- **1 tablespoon olive oil**
- **juice of 1 large lime**
- **4 teaspoons snipped fresh chives**
- **4 teaspoons minced fresh chervil or parsley**
- **coarse salt and white pepper**

If you have sea scallops, cut each into quarters. Rinse scallops and roll in paper towels to dry thoroughly. Put the toast triangles on 6 warmed plates and keep them warm, not hot. Heat butter and oil in a large skillet. When very hot, dump in the scallops all at once and sauté them for 2 minutes. With wooden spoons turn them to sauté on all sides, as much as possible, for about 2 minutes longer. Pour in the lime juice and sprinkle in chives, chervil or parsley, and a pinch each of coarse salt and white pepper. All this should be done within 6 minutes. Gently stir to mix all ingredients, then divide the scallops and all the pan juices among the toast triangles.

Spaghetti with White Clam Sauce

4 portions as a first course

- **3 dozen Little Neck or Cherrystone clams**
- **2 garlic cloves**
- **¼ cup olive oil**
- **1 small dried hot red pepper**
- **8 ounces uncooked spaghetti**
- **2 tablespoons butter**
- **black pepper**
- **3 tablespoons chopped parsley**

Scrub the clams. Peel garlic cloves and put through a press. Heat the oil in a large saucepan and add the garlic and red pepper. Cook over moderately low heat until garlic begins to brown, 1 to 2 minutes. Add the clams, cover, and increase the heat to moderately high. Cook, shaking the pan frequently, until the clams open, 6 to 8 minutes. Remove from the heat, remove clams from shells, and set aside covered. Strain the cooking liquid through a fine-mesh sieve lined with dampened cheesecloth into a clean saucepan.

Meanwhile, boil the spaghetti (see Volume 4 Index) in a large pot of salted water until *al dente,* tender but still slightly resistant to the bite, 8 to 12 minutes. Drain pasta and toss with the butter in a heated serving bowl. Briefly reheat the clams in their cooking liquid and pour over the spaghetti. Sprinkle with freshly ground pepper to taste and the chopped parsley. Toss to mix and serve hot.

Shrimp Creole

4 portions

1½ pounds medium shrimps
2 celery ribs
2 large onions
3 cloves garlic
1 large green bell pepper
1¾ cups canned peeled tomatoes
2 tablespoons olive oil
1 cup dry white wine
1 teaspoon salt
1 teaspoon sugar
1 tablespoon red-wine vinegar
1 tablespoon cornstarch
few drops Tabasco sauce

Rinse the raw shrimps, then shell and devein them. Wash and dry celery and mince both ribs and any leaves. Peel and mince onions and garlic. Wash and halve pepper, discard stem, seeds and ribs, and chop pepper. Drain the canned tomatoes and chop them. Heat the oil in a large deep skillet or flameproof casserole over moderate heat. Add celery and onions and cook until onions are soft and translucent but not browned, 4 to 6 minutes. Pour the wine into the pan, reduce heat to low, and simmer for 10 minutes, stirring occasionally. Add the chopped tomatoes, salt, sugar and vinegar. Simmer for 10 minutes longer, stirring occasionally. Add green pepper and simmer for another 10 minutes.

Stir the cornstarch into ¼ cup cold water, and mix into the sauce, stirring. Increase heat to moderate, bring the sauce to a boil, and cook, stirring, until it is thickened, about 2 minutes. Add Tabasco sauce to taste. Add the shrimps and cook until they are pink and curled, about 2 minutes longer. Serve over a bed of rice.

Scallops in Tomato and Cream Sauce

6 to 8 portions

This recipe can be prepared in stages. The court bouillon can be made a day ahead. The scallops and tomato mixture can be prepared several hours ahead and refrigerated separately, along with the sauce base. Reheat gently before proceeding with the recipe.

Court Bouillon

- 1 large onion
- 3 garlic cloves
- 1 bouquet garni (4 parsley sprigs, 6 peppercorns, 6 allspice berries, ½ teaspoon dried thyme, 1 bay leaf)
- ½ cup white-wine vinegar
- 1½ cups water
- ¼ teaspoon salt
- ½ teaspoon Worcestershire sauce

Make the court bouillon: Peel and chop the onion. Peel and crush the garlic. Tie all ingredients for the *bouquet garni* in a square of cheesecloth. Put all the ingredients in a nonaluminum saucepan. Bring to a boil over high heat, then reduce heat to low, cover, and simmer for 25 minutes. Strain, pressing down on the vegetables and *bouquet garni* to extract as much flavor as possible; discard vegetables and *bouquet garni.* If you have made this in advance, refrigerate it.

Scallops and Tomato Mixture

- 2 pounds bay scallops
- 1 shallot
- 4 medium-size tomatoes
- 4 ounces plus 1½ tablespoons butter
- ½ teaspoon salt
- ½ teaspoon white pepper
- 1 teaspoon cornstarch
- ¼ cup heavy cream
- 4 egg yolks
- 1 teaspoon lemon juice
- parsley sprigs, for garnish
- 6 lemon wedges
- 12 croutons of fried bread (optional)

Pour the court bouillon into a saucepan and bring it to a simmer. Add the scallops and cook over low heat for about 3 minutes, until they are tender and just opaque throughout. Remove scallops with a slotted spoon and set aside. Boil the court bouillon over high heat until reduced to ½ cup. Remove from heat and cool to lukewarm.

Peel and mince the shallot. Blanch and peel the tomatoes and chop them; remove as many seeds as possible. Melt 1½ tablespoons of the butter in a small heavy saucepan over low heat. Add the minced shallot and cook, stirring, for 1 minute, until softened. Add the tomatoes and stir to mix. Increase heat to moderate and cook for 5 minutes, until most of the juice of the tomatoes has evaporated. Season with half of the salt and pepper and remove from heat.

Whisk the cornstarch and cream together until blended, then whisk the mixture into the lukewarm court bouillon. Beat in the egg yolks, one at a time. Whisk the mixture for about 1 minute. If it is at all lumpy, strain it. Set the pan over very low heat and cook, stirring constantly with the whisk, until the sauce thickens enough to coat the wires of the whisk lightly. Do not let the sauce boil or it may curdle. Remove from heat.

Melt remaining 4 ounces butter in a small saucepan over moderate heat. Set the pan containing the sauce on a dampened potholder to keep it steady. Very slowly whisk the melted butter into the sauce, a few drops at a time, beating constantly. When all the butter has been added, stir in remaining salt and pepper and the lemon juice. Gently stir in the tomato mixture. Taste, and add more salt and pepper if necessary.

Add the scallops to the tomato and cream sauce. Warm gently over low heat for 1 to 2 minutes, until heated through. Pour over a bed of rice on a warmed serving dish. Decorate with parsley sprigs and lemon wedges, and the croutons if desired. Serve hot.

Crab au Gratin

4 portions

1 medium-size onion
2 celery ribs
4 ounces mushrooms
3 tablespoons butter
1 tablespoon crème fraîche or heavy cream
few drops of Worcestershire sauce
1 cup Béchamel Sauce (see Volume 3 Index)
1 pound lump crab meat
salt and black pepper
1 ounce Parmesan cheese, grated (1/4 cup)
2 tablespoons fresh white bread crumbs
parsley sprigs
several cooked shrimps, for garnish

Peel and mince the onion. Wash and dry the celery and cut into thin slices. Wipe mushrooms with a damp cloth, trim base of stems, and cut caps and stems into thin slices. Preheat oven to 375°F. Melt 2 tablespoons of the butter in a skillet over moderate heat. Cook the onion and celery in the butter, stirring occasionally, until onion is softened but not browned, 4 to 5 minutes. Add the mushrooms and cook, tossing frequently, for 2 minutes longer.

Whisk the *crème fraîche* or heavy cream and the Worcestershire sauce into the béchamel sauce. Add the sautéed vegetables and their juices and stir to mix. Gently fold in the crab meat. Season with salt and pepper to taste.

Turn the mixture into a buttered gratin dish or 4 individual ramekins. Sprinkle the top with the cheese and bread crumbs. Dot with remaining 1 tablespoon butter. Bake in the preheated oven for about 15 minutes, until the mixture is hot all through and the top is golden brown. Decorate with parsley and a few shrimps.

Variations: Bake flaky pastry in scallop shells. Serve the crab mixture in these pastry cases.

Mix cooked rice and peas together and pack into a ring mold; turn out. Fill the center with the crab mixture. Omit cheese and bread crumbs and serve without reheating.

Use the crab mixture as a vol-au-vent filling; omit the cheese and bread crumbs. Fill small chou puffs (see Volume 4) with the crab mixture.

Scalloped Oysters

6 portions

- **2 pints shucked oysters with liquor**
- **4 ounces unsalted butter**
- **4 large pimientos**
- **3 cups crumbled unsalted crackers**
- **1 cup heavy cream**
- **salt and white pepper**

Turn oysters into a large strainer set over a bowl. Check oysters to remove any bits of shell. Melt the butter in a small pan over low heat. Rinse the pimientos to remove any seeds and packing juice and cut them into thin strips. Preheat oven to 350°F. Butter a shallow 2-quart baking dish. Combine oysters and pimientos. Sprinkle 1 cup of the cracker crumbs over the dish and add half of the oysters and pimientos. Sprinkle with about half of the melted butter. Sprinkle in another cup of crumbs, then the rest of the oysters and pimientos. Sprinkle with the rest of the melted butter. Top with remaining crumbs. Combine the cream with ½ cup of the oyster liquor and season it with salt and pepper. Slowly pour the cream into the dish, around the edges. The liquid should reach the second layer of oysters. If it does not, add more cream and oyster liquor. Bake in the oven for 35 to 45 minutes, until the juices are bubbling around the edges, the top is lightly browned, and the oysters are puffed up.

Coquilles Saint-Jacques

(Scallops and Mushrooms in White-Wine Sauce and Cheese)

4 portions

- **7 tablespoons butter**
- **1½ pounds sea scallops**
- **4 ounces mushrooms**
- **2 shallots**
- **¾ cup dry white wine**
- **¾ teaspoon salt**
- **½ teaspoon plus ⅛ teaspoon white pepper**
- **6 black peppercorns**
- **1 bay leaf**
- **3 parsley sprigs**
- **1½ tablespoons all-purpose flour**
- **¾ cup milk**
- **2 egg yolks**
- **½ cup heavy cream**
- **¼ teaspoon grated nutmeg**
- **1 teaspoon lemon juice**
- **1½ ounces Gruyère cheese, grated (⅓ cup)**

Coat 4 scallop shells or a flameproof gratin dish with 2 tablespoons of the butter. Cut the scallops crosswise into ¼-inch slices. Wipe mushrooms with a damp cloth and trim base of stems; slice caps and stems. Peel and mince the shallots.

Pour the wine into a heavy nonaluminum saucepan and add the scallops, mushrooms, ½ teaspoon of the salt, ½ teaspoon of the white pepper, the black peppercorns, the bay leaf, parsley and minced shallots. Add water, if necessary, barely to cover the scallops. Bring to a simmer over moderate heat. Reduce heat to low, cover the pan, and simmer for 5 minutes. With a slotted spoon remove scallops and mushrooms to a bowl. Boil the liquid in the pan until reduced by one third. Strain through a fine sieve and measure out ¾ cup. Discard the flavorings and the extra liquid.

Make the sauce: Melt 3 tablespoons of the butter in a heavy saucepan over low heat. Stir in the flour and cook, stirring, for 2 minutes, without letting the flour color, to make a roux. Gradually whisk in the ¾ cup reduced scallop cooking liquid and the milk. Bring to a boil, reduce heat and simmer, stirring frequently, for 5 minutes, until the sauce is thickened and smooth. Remove sauce from heat.

In a small bowl beat the egg yolks with the cream until blended. Whisk a little of the hot sauce into the egg-yolk and cream mixture to warm it. Slowly whisk the warmed liaison into the rest of the sauce. Cook over low heat, stirring, for 1 to 2 minutes, until sauce is heated through and thickened. Add remaining ¼ teaspoon salt and ⅛ teaspoon white pepper, the nutmeg and lemon juice. Fold in the scallops and mushrooms.

Preheat the broiler. Spoon the scallop mixture into the buttered scallop shells. Sprinkle the grated cheese over the top. Melt remaining 2 tablespoons butter and drizzle over the cheese. Broil for about 3 minutes, until cheese is melted and the top is browned and sizzling. Serve immediately.

Variation: For a professional finish, pipe a border of duchesse potatoes around the edge of the scallop shells before you put them under the broiler to brown. If you pipe it around before spooning the scallop mixture into the shells, it will serve to keep the mixture from spilling over, in addition to looking so appetizing.

Seafood Mayonnaise

4 portions

- **1 lobster, about 1½ pounds**
- **8 ounces firm-textured white fish (cod, halibut, tilefish)**
- **8 ounces cooked medium shrimps**
- **1 egg yolk, at room temperature**
- **¼ teaspoon salt**
- **⅛ teaspoon white pepper**
- **½ teaspoon paprika**
- **1 teaspoon prepared Dijon-style mustard**
- **2 teaspoons lemon juice**
- **10 tablespoons olive oil or vegetable oil**
- **1 tablespoon snipped fresh chives**
- **1 tablespoon capers**
- **½ large cucumber**
- **2 large tomatoes**

Boil the lobster and cool it. Remove lobster meat from the shell and chop it. Poach the fish until just tender. Cool it. Remove any bones or skin and flake the fish. Shell and devein the shrimps. Place lobster, fish and shrimps in a mixing bowl. Cover the bowl and refrigerate the seafood while you make a mayonnaise.

In a small mixing bowl combine the egg yolk, salt, white pepper, paprika, mustard and 1 teaspoon of the lemon juice. Using a wire whisk, beat the ingredients until well blended. Add the oil, a few drops at a time, whisking constantly. Do not add the oil too quickly or the mayonnaise will curdle. After the mayonnaise has thickened, the oil may be added a little more rapidly. Beat in a few drops of lemon juice from time to time to keep the mayonnaise from becoming too thick. When all the oil has been added, stir in any remaining lemon juice. Taste, and add more salt and pepper if needed. Stir in the chives and the capers.

Peel cucumber and tomatoes and cut both into thin slices. Remove seafood mixture from refrigerator and fold in the mayonnaise. Arrange cucumber and tomato slices around a large serving dish and pile the seafood mayonnaise in the center. Cover and chill in the refrigerator for at least 20 minutes before serving.

Boiled Lobster

4 portions

4 live lobsters, 1 to 1½ pounds each
6 ounces unsalted butter
lemon wedges

Bring a large lobster pot or stockpot of salted water to a rolling boil over high heat. Plunge the lobsters in head first, cover the pot tightly, and cook for 10 to 15 minutes, until the shells are bright red and the tail meat is opaque throughout, but still tender and juicy.

Remove lobsters from the pot to a board and split them lengthwise down the underside; be careful, because a lot of juices may come pouring out. Remove the intestinal tract. Use a teaspoon to dig out the sand sac in the head in one piece. Leave any red coral or green tomalley in place.

Melt the butter over low heat; skim off the foam from the top, and pour it carefully into a clean vessel, leaving the creamy residue at the bottom of the pan. This is clarified butter. Divide the butter among 4 small bowls. Serve the lobster with the butter and lemon wedges.

Broiled Lobster

2 portions

2 live lobsters, 1 to 1½ pounds each
4 tablespoons unsalted butter, softened
salt and black pepper
melted butter
lemon wedges

Preheat the broiler or light the charcoal under a grill. Kill the lobsters and split them lengthwise. When the broiler is hot, place the lobster halves, cut sides down, on a buttered broiler or grill rack. Broil or grill the lobster for 8 minutes.

Turn lobster halves over and brush liberally with about half of the softened butter. Season lightly with salt and pepper. Continue to cook for 6 to 8 minutes longer, brushing with more of the butter every 2 or 3 minutes. The lobsters are done when the shells are bright red and the meat is opaque throughout, but still juicy and tender. Serve with melted butter and lemon wedges.

Deviled Lobster

2 main-course portions or 4 first-course portions

2 tablespoons Worcestershire sauce
1 tablespoon tomato purée, or 1½ teaspoons tomato paste
1 tablespoon tarragon vinegar
1 teaspoon minced onion
1 tablespoon fresh lemon juice
1 teaspoon salt
½ teaspoon black pepper
1 bay leaf
¼ cup dry red wine
1 garlic clove
4 large mushrooms
3 tomatoes
2 live lobsters, 1 pound each
4 ounces butter
¼ cup brandy
½ cup heavy cream
parsley sprigs, for garnish

In a medium-size, nonaluminum saucepan combine the Worcestershire sauce, tomato purée, vinegar, onion, lemon juice, salt, pepper, bay leaf and wine. Peel garlic and put through a press into the mixture. Wipe mushrooms with a damp cloth, trim base of stems, and cut caps and stems into thin slices. Blanch and peel the tomatoes and chop them; discard as many seeds as possible. Add mushrooms and tomatoes to the saucepan. Bring to a boil over high heat, reduce heat to low, and simmer the sauce, stirring occasionally, for 15 minutes. Remove from the heat and set aside to cool. Remove and discard the bay leaf. Preheat oven to 375°F.

Kill lobsters and split them lengthwise. Remove intestinal tract and the sand sac in the head. Melt the butter in a large flameproof casserole over moderate heat. Add the lobster halves and cook, turning the lobsters and basting them with the butter, until the shells turn bright red, about 5 minutes. Add the brandy to the pan, warm it for a few moments, then ignite it with a long match. Shake the pan over heat until the flames subside. Cover the casserole and transfer it to the oven. Bake the lobster for 10 minutes.

Meanwhile, reheat the sauce until boiling. Arrange the cooked lobster halves, cut sides up, on a warmed platter. Crack the claws if desired. Strain any juices from the casserole into the sauce. Stir in the cream. If the sauce is very thin, boil it to reduce it slightly. Check the seasoning. Spoon the hot sauce liberally over the lobsters. Garnish the platter with parsley sprigs. Pass any remaining sauce separately.

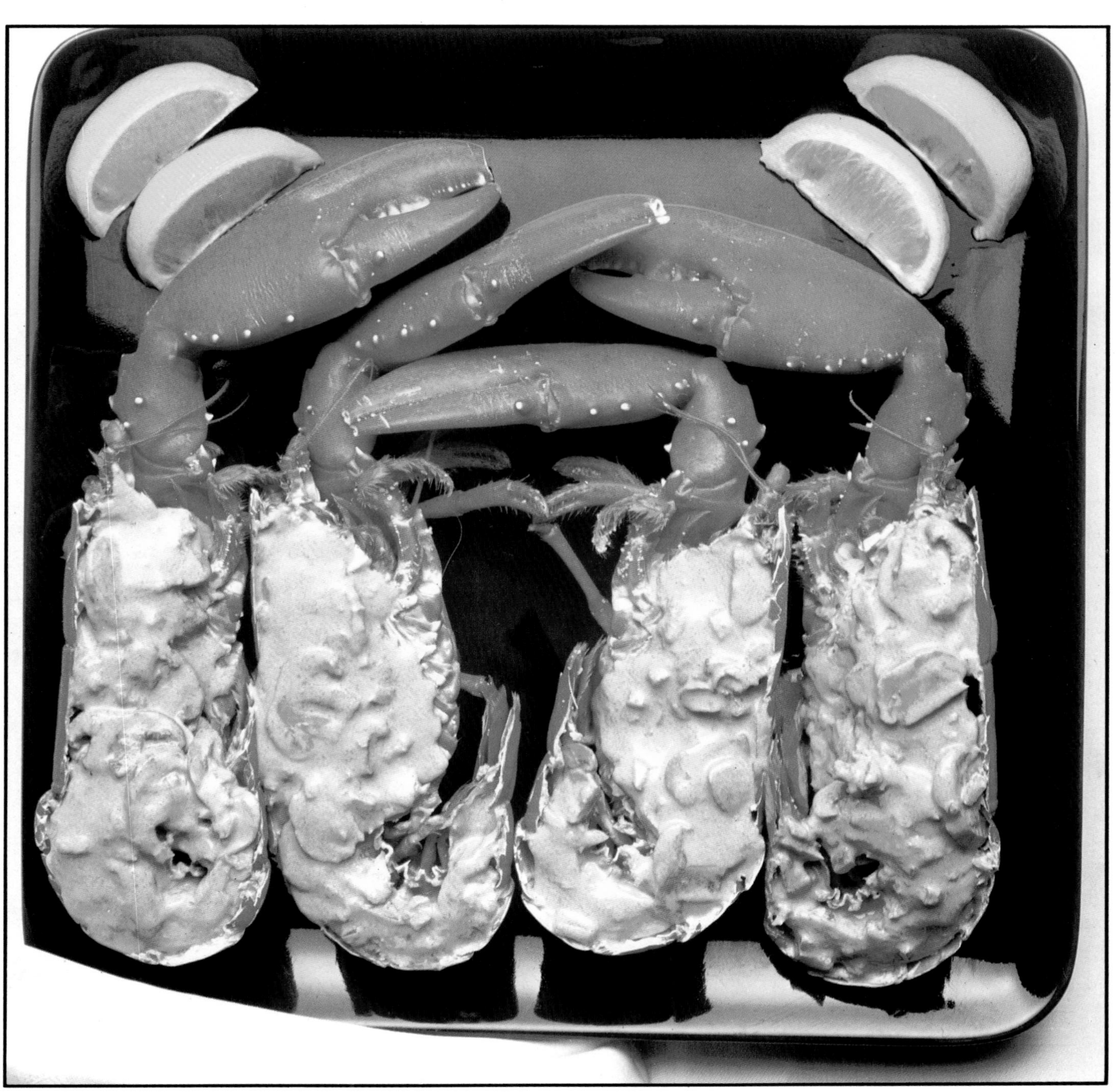

Rémoulade Sauce

makes 1 ¼ cups

- **1 hard-cooked egg**
- **1 garlic clove**
- **1 ¼ cups Mayonnaise (see Volume 3 Index)**
- **1 teaspoon anchovy paste**
- **1 teaspoon minced fresh parsley**
- **½ tablespoon capers**
- **½ teaspoon dried tarragon**

Peel and mince the hard-cooked egg. Peel the garlic and put through a press into the egg. Add mayonnaise, anchovy paste, parsley, capers, and tarragon and mix well. Refrigerate and use within 2 days.

Crab-Meat Salad with Rémoulade Sauce

4 portions

- **1 pound cooked crab meat, fresh or canned**
- **1 large head of Boston lettuce**
- **4 firm tomatoes**
- **1 ripe avocado**
- **lemon juice**
- **½ cucumber**
- **12 pitted black olives**
- **1 ¼ cups Rémoulade Sauce (preceding recipe)**

Remove any shell or cartilage from the crab meat. Wash the lettuce and separate into leaves; dry leaves and arrange them around the edge of a large serving dish. Blanch and peel tomatoes and cut into slices. Peel avocado, halve it, discard the pit, and cut the fruit lengthwise into slices. Brush the slices on both sides with lemon juice to prevent discoloring. Peel cucumber and cut into thin slices.

Put the crab in the center of the lettuce-lined dish. Arrange slices of tomato, avocado and cucumber around the crab and the olives in the curves of the avocado slices. Spoon rémoulade sauce over the crab; or serve the sauce separately in a sauceboat; or, if you prefer, mix the crab with the sauce before arranging it on the serving dish.

Shrimps en Cocotte

4 portions

- **8 ounces shrimps**
- **1 small fennel bulb**
- **1 medium-size shallot**
- **1 cup dry white wine**
- **⅛ teaspoon mace**
- **1 small bay leaf**
- **6 black peppercorns**
- **½ cup milk**
- **1 teaspoon fennel seeds**
- **2 tablespoons plus 2 teaspoons butter**
- **2 tablespoons flour**
- **½ cup fish stock or bottled clam broth**
- **3 tablespoons heavy cream**
- **salt and black pepper**
- **fresh white bread crumbs**

Shell and devein the shrimps. Trim the fennel, discard the tough stems and any coarse or damaged outer ribs, and cut the bulb into strips about ½ inch thick. Peel and chop the shallot. Pour the wine into a small nonaluminum saucepan. Add the chopped shallot, the mace, bay leaf and peppercorns, and boil until the liquid is reduced to ½ cup. Strain the infusion and set aside.

Pour the milk into another small saucepan and add the fennel seeds. Steep them over low heat for 15 minutes; strain, reserving the milk. Return the milk to the saucepan, add the fennel strips, and bring to a simmer. Poach the fennel until softened, 5 to 10 minutes. With a slotted spoon, transfer fennel to 4 buttered individual ramekins, dividing it evenly; reserve the milk. Divide the shrimps among the ramekins.

Make a velouté sauce: Melt 2 tablespoons of the butter in a medium-size saucepan. Add the flour and cook over moderate heat, stirring, until the flour begins to turn a pale straw color. Remove from heat and whisk in the fish stock and the reserved wine infusion and the milk. Bring to a boil, stirring; reduce heat and simmer for 3 minutes. Add the cream and season with salt and pepper to taste. Pour this sauce over the shrimps and fennel.

To complete the dish, preheat oven to 400°F. Sprinkle bread crumbs over the tops of the ramekins and dot with remaining butter. Bake for 15 minutes, until the crumbs are golden and the sauce is bubbling.

Stuffed Clams

4 portions

- **12 medium-size chowder clams**
- **4 strips of bacon**
- **2 medium-size onions**
- **2½ cups fresh white bread crumbs**
- **¼ cup minced fresh parsley**
- **1 tablespoon grated lemon rind**
- **Tabasco or Worcestershire sauce**

Scrub the clams. Steam them open in a large kettle with about 1 inch of water. Reserve 12 half-shells and scrub them; discard the rest. Strain the broth through a fine-mesh sieve lined with several layers of dampened cheesecloth; set aside. Chop the clams, by hand or in a food processor fitted with the steel blade. The pieces should be about the size of dried lentils.

Cook the bacon in a skillet until crisp. Remove, cool, and crumble the bacon. Pour off all but 1 tablespoon of the bacon fat. Peel and mince the onions and sauté them in the skillet until translucent. Still over heat, stir in 2 cups of the bread crumbs, the parsley and lemon rind. Remove pan from heat and stir in the chopped clams and the crumbled bacon. Add some of the reserved clam broth to make the mixture moist but not soupy. Add Tabasco or Worcestershire to taste.

Spoon the mixture into the reserved 12 shells. Sprinkle remaining bread crumbs over the tops, dividing them evenly. Set the clams in a baking pan, nestling them in a bed of coarse salt or propping them up with crumpled foil if necessary. Bake them in a preheated 400°F oven for 15 to 20 minutes, until the tops are golden brown and crisp. Serve 3 clams per portion as a main course.

Part Three
YEAST BREADS

"The smell of good bread baking, like the sound of flowing water, is indescribable in its evocation of innocence and delight."

—M. F. K. Fisher

In the entire realm of food and drink, there is nothing more basic than bread. Throughout history, bread has often been used to represent nourishment itself: when we sit down with someone to enjoy a meal, we are said to "break bread." The original meaning of the word "companion" was "one to share bread with." We even see bread's place as an elemental commodity in the familiar slang terms "bread" and "dough," both used to refer to money.

There is something warm and reassuring about the aroma of bread baking in the oven. If you have never tried bread making, you will be surprised at how simple it is, and you will discover there's nothing like the satisfaction of kneading, baking and eating your own homebaked bread.

Over the years there has developed a mystique around bread making that has most of us intimidated. Either we imagine that making bread is difficult or strenuous, or we think it requires hours and hours for endless risings. Nothing could be further from the truth.

Basically, all you need to make bread are four simple ingredients: flour, water, yeast and salt. Flour provides structure, water lends moisture, yeast raises the dough, and salt adds flavor, as well as checking the action of the yeast. Most of the time involved in preparing bread dough is spent in unsupervised rising, and few people realize that bread rises best slowly at a cool temperature, so there's no need to plan hours and hours at home for baking. A dough can be thrown together quickly, kneaded, then refrigerated overnight and baked the next day while you attend to other chores.

Although few of us could compete with Tobias Smollett when he wrote proudly in 1771, "My bread is sweet and nourishing, made from my own wheat, ground in my own mill, and baked in my own oven," we can come very close.

Many good flours are now available nationally, as more home cooks try their hands at homemade bread. Many electric mixers come equipped with a dough hook that makes kneading effortless, though the old expression, *"il faut mettre les mains à la pâte"* (one must get one's hands right into the dough) might just be true. There's nothing like kneading dough by hand to get a feel for the real joy of working with food, and it's a great way to get rid of pent-up aggression, too.

Homebaked bread is fresher, more nutritious and more delicious than the commercial product. It freezes well, which can increase the dividends of your labor over a period of time.

The history of bread making goes back as far as recorded time. Many of the basic grains and baking methods have not changed radically since the days of the Romans. Visitors to Pompeii can see a combined mill and bakery from the first century A.D., which once processed 1,000 bushels of flour (for 100,000 to 150,000 loaves) every day. The brick oven in Pompeii is similar to the kind used for centuries and similar ones can be found in numerous American homes from early Colonial days.

For many centuries, bread baking was such an important part of commerce that it was controlled by strict official regulations. In Germany, bakers would give customers an extra roll or bun to avoid punishment in the stocks for giving too little—hence the term "baker's dozen."

As bread became more of a commercial product, and as people demanded whiter bread as a sign of their increasing refinement, quality inexorably declined. Fortunately for us, the homebaked article is well within our grasp.

Breads fall into two main groups: *quick breads* such as muffins, tea breads and popovers, which are raised with chemical leavens such as baking powder and bicarbonate of soda, and *yeast breads.* It is the latter with which we are concerned here.

Yeast is a living organism, and its action on bread is nothing short of miraculous. Early bakers did not know how yeast worked, but they did know that a piece of yesterday's risen bread dough would help today's batch to rise. Bread was usually leavened with a *barm,* or a mash of grain, flour or potatoes, which provided a fertile environment for natural yeasts found in the air. In Chaucer's day, yeast was called *goddisgoode,* since it was a gift of the grace of God.

Yeast is available to us fresh or dried, and in either form it contains millions of active living cells per ounce. When given a moist, warm environment in which to grow, such as bread dough, yeast converts starch into sugar and releases carbon dioxide, which causes the dough to rise. Sugar feeds yeast, and is often used to help get it started, but this is unnecessary. In fact, most recipes call for too much yeast; the longer the dough rises, the less yeast is needed. The slightly acid flavor bestowed by the yeast is an important part of the delicious flavor that characterizes freshly baked bread.

Yeast must not be added to liquid that is too hot (130° or higher), or it will be killed; but if the liquid is under 80°, the yeast will remain dormant. The optimal temperature for yeast is 105° to 115°F, or just above body heat. The term *proof,* which means to rise, originally referred to a test to prove that the yeast was active. Today's yeast needs no such test unless it has been on the shelf for a very long time. Sometimes the yeast is added to a portion of the flour with the liquid to get the fermentation started; this is called a *sponge.*

For many years white bread was just about everyone's only conception of bread. Now we realize that bread made with at least a portion of whole wheat or other whole grain contains more protein and fiber than white bread. Even more important, it tastes better. That other grains are very much in vogue is evidenced by the many people who are actually grinding their own grains because they want a truly old-fashioned flavor.

To appreciate the differences between types of bread, we must understand the composition of a kernel of wheat. Each grain of wheat, which has been called a "complex little storehouse," contains the *wheat germ,* which is the embryo, comprising 2% of the grain. The germ is rich in protein, vitamins, oils and flavor. The outer protective layers of the kernel are the *bran,* with valuable fiber, forming 13% of the grain. The remaining 85% of the wheat kernel is the starchy *endosperm,* the heart of the grain. White flour contains only the starch, with none of the nutrients, fiber or flavor found in the germ or the bran. Whole-wheat flour consists of 100% of the wheat kernel, in ground form.

Many varieties of flour are now widely available. Unless you bake constantly, it's best to buy flours in small quantities to insure freshness. White flour is the easiest to find, and the unbleached variety is the best choice. Responding to the increasing interest in bread baking, manufacturers now market bread flour, which has a higher gluten content, about 14%, than all-purpose flour. Gluten is the protein that gives bread its strength and elasticity, making the structure firm as the yeast gives it height. Bread flour absorbs more liquid than all-purpose flour, and may require more kneading. In any case, flour amounts must always be approximate when baking bread. As you knead the dough, sprinkle on a bit more flour any time the dough feels sticky.

Whole-grain flours, such as whole wheat, graham (whole wheat with the bran in coarser granules), rye, barley, oat flour and others, will give distinctive flavor and texture to your breads. Because whole-grain flours are somewhat heavy, they are best combined with a portion of unbleached white flour, for a lighter-textured bread. Stone-ground flour is flour that has been milled by stone rather than by mechanical rollers. These flours can spoil quickly, and should be covered and stored carefully.

There is no special equipment to buy for baking bread. Loaves can be fashioned free-form on a baking sheet, or you can use glass, metal or ceramic loaf pans, or other baking pans. Black steel pans help make a crusty loaf by reflecting the heat onto the dough. Clay loaf pans also make good bread. Empty cans are useful for tall breads, such as a *brioche parisienne.* Springform pans make hearty round loaves similar to the festive cakes baked in hoops in past centuries. An electric mixer or food processor is a help in kneading dough, but is certainly not essential. In France, baskets called *bannetons* are used to hold the dough while rising, but, of course, any bowl will do.

Bernard Clayton, Jr., who has written several excellent books on the subject of baking bread, offers the following reassuring advice: "Baking is a relaxed art. There is no step in the bread-making process that cannot, in some way, be delayed or moved ahead just a bit to make it more convenient to fit into a busy schedule. If you are called away overnight just when the dough is rising in the pans, oil the dough surfaces, cover with plastic wrap and slip the pans in the refrigerator to keep until you return. If the dough you are shaping gets stubborn, pulls back and refuses to be shaped, walk away from it for a few minutes. It will relax, and so will you."

On the other hand, he says, "Don't baby the dough. Break the kneading rhythm by occasionally throwing the dough down hard against the work surface. Wham! Don't gentle it! Smack it down hard!" *(The Breads of France)*

In other words, relax, have fun, and get to know your dough. Yeast dough is a living thing and the better you get to know it, the better your bread will be.

YEAST BREADS

Making yeast bread is one of the most rewarding of all baking experiences. Bread making is not difficult, but it is important to familiarize yourself with the characteristics of the major ingredients you'll be working with.

Flour

Flours are defined by the "rate of extraction." This means the percentage of the whole grain left in after the flour has been milled. The name of the flour is a guide to the amount of whole grain it contains.

Flours are also defined by the type of wheat from which they are extracted, i.e., "hard" and "soft" wheat. Hard wheat is higher in gluten than soft wheat, therefore hard wheat flour is better for bread making. Gluten is a "rubbery" grain protein that reacts with water and yeast, makes the dough strong and elastic, and enables it to expand with the growth of the yeast and the bubbles it makes.

The following flours are the most commonly used:

Whole Wheat. These flours contain the whole of the cleaned wheat grain, nothing added and nothing taken away. Bread made with these will have a good nutty flavor and close texture. For a lighter texture with the good flavor of whole meal, use half whole wheat and half white flour.

Because it contains the whole germ of the wheat, the fat content is higher in whole-wheat flour. Storage in the refrigerator is recommended. Whole-wheat *pastry* flour is often found in health-food stores. It is made from soft wheat and is not recommended for bread making.

White Flour. This flour is made from a mixture of hard wheat and soft wheat and is divided into different types: *unbleached,* somewhat creamy in color and labeled all-purpose, and *bleached* flour. Bleached flour is bleached by aging, not by chemicals. Both flours are "enriched." This means that some of the nutrients that were removed to make the flour white have been restored to it. Although both unbleached and bleached flour are labeled "all-purpose," unbleached flour contains more gluten and is therefore better for bread making.

Cake Flour. This is made from soft wheat and has a lower gluten content. Cake flour comes in two forms: self-rising, which contains a leavening or raising agent such as baking powder, and plain cake flour, which contains no leavening agent. If a bread recipe calls for the addition of a small amount of cake flour, be sure it is *not* self-rising.

Bread Flour. Some flour companies are now producing a flour with a higher gluten content, called "bread flour." This is a white flour that gives excellent results.

Gluten Flour. This flour can be found in health-food stores although it is quite expensive. Extremely high in protein (almost 4 times the amount of protein in regular flour), its high gluten content gives lightness when used in combination with whole-grain flours, such as whole wheat and rye.

Rye Flour. This is lower in gluten than wheat flours. Because it inhibits the rise induced by yeast, it is never used alone but in combination with other flours that have a higher and more stable gluten content.

Soy Flour. This flour is very high in protein and adds nutritive value to baked goods. Since it contains no gluten and also has a rather strong flavor, it is used only in small quantities and combined with other flours. A good rule of thumb is to use no more than 3 tablespoons soy flour for each cup of wheat flour.

Triticale Flour. A comparatively recent development in the flour world, this is made from a hybrid of wheat and rye and is supposedly higher in protein than either. It too should be used in combination with other flours that have a higher gluten content.

Other Grains. Other ingredients, such as wheat germ, bran, oats, corn meal, cracked wheat (bulgur), can be added to flour in bread making but only in small quantities since they contain no gluten and would make an overly dense loaf.

Yeast

This is the agent that makes bread rise. Yeast is a living plant that needs food and comfort. The food is supplied by the other ingredients in the bread recipe and the comfort by the warm temperatures. As yeast grows, it gives off carbon dioxide, which expands. As it does, the elastic cell walls of the gluten stretch to form the risen structure.

Yeast is found in two forms: dried granular yeast and fresh compressed yeast cakes. Dried granular yeast is sold in individual packets or envelopes of ¼ ounce each, or in jars and packets that contain from 4 to 16 ounces. The individual packet contains a scant tablespoon of yeast. The packet or 1 tablespoon of yeast is equivalent to 1 cake of fresh compressed yeast (0.6 ounces). Fresh yeast is sold in small blocks of 0.6 ounce each or in a large 2-ounce package. Fresh yeast is extremely perishable and increasingly hard to find. Even if it is perfectly fresh when purchased, it will have a limited life even under refrigeration.

Granulated yeast will last for months under refrigeration. If you buy the yeast in individual packets, open them and put them in a small screw-top jar in the refrigerator. This will give you greater flexibility when using whole grains as you will need to adjust the amount of yeast, depending on the proportion of whole-meal flours and grains, etc.

To use either kind of yeast, there are four possible methods:

Dissolved Yeast Method. Fresh or dried yeast is dissolved in warm liquid. Fresh yeast is crumbled into liquid (80° to 90°F); dry yeast is sprinkled into liquid (110° to 115°F). Dissolve a little sugar in the warm liquid before adding dry yeast. When the liquid is frothy, add it to flour, or add flour to liquid, according to the recipe.

Sponge Batter Method. Combine yeast with a third of the total amount of flour needed for the recipe, the entire quantity of liquid and 1 teaspoon of sugar, to make a batter. The batter mixture will froth up like a sponge in about 20 minutes. This is useful for dry yeast.

Rubbed-in Method. Use this one with fresh yeast. Break up yeast, add to flour, and rub yeast in with fingertips until the bits are well dispersed. Add fat and liquid in the usual way.

Rapid Mix Method. Use this with dry yeast. Mix yeast with some or all of the dry ingredients of the recipe. Add liquids at 120° to 125°F. Follow usual method for rising.

No matter which method you use, the temperature of the liquid is critical for success. Use a yeast or dairy thermometer to be accurate. If you lack a thermometer, combine boiling water with an equal amount of ice water. This will approximate the 105°F to 115°F necessary for *granulated* yeast. You should be able to hold your finger in it for the count of ten without any discomfort. The lower temperature of 80°F to 90°F necessary for *fresh* yeast is harder to estimate without a thermometer. It is important to remember that a temperature too high will kill the yeast. A temperature too low will make the yeast sluggish and will take longer to foam up. When the liquid in which the yeast is dissolved becomes foamy and frothy, it means that the yeast has been "proofed," i.e., it has proved it is alive.

Granulated yeast will not "proof" in plain water; it needs a bit of sugar or sweetener to activate it. Many recipes call for more sugar than is necessary. As little as 1/4 teaspoon of sugar is enough to stimulate the yeast to grow.

The liquid used to dissolve the yeast may be water or milk.

Liquids

Liquids for bread making may be water, milk, a combination of both of

Food Processor Bread

Makes 2 loaves

- **1 package active dry yeast**
- **1/4 cup warm water (105° to 115°F)**
- **1 cup hot tap water**
- **1/2 cup (1 stick) butter, cut into 8 pieces**
- **2 tablespoons sugar**
- **2 teaspoons salt**
- **3/4 cup warm water**
- **5-7 cups unbleached all-purpose flour**

1 **Dissolve yeast in 1/4 cup warm water. Pour hot water over butter, sugar and salt in small bowl.**

2 **Metal blade in place, add 3/4 cup warm water, 3 cups flour and yeast mixture to work bowl. Process several seconds until mixed.**

3 **Add butter mixture and 1 cup of the remaining flour. Process briefly.**

4 **Of the remaining flour, add 1 cup at a time, just until a soft dough is formed.**

- Food processor kneading takes no more than 1 minutes. Do not overprocess.
- Remove dough from work bowl. Shape into a ball and place in oiled bowl. Cover; leave in warm place and allow to rise until dough is doubled.
- Proceed to follow standard baking procedure, as outlined in directions for traditional bread.

French Bread

2 bâtards or 4 baguettes

1 envelope active dry yeast (1 scant tablespoon),
or 1 package fresh yeast
1 cup warm water
1 teaspoon sugar
4 to 5 cups all-purpose flour
2 teaspoons salt

This dough may be shaped in various ways. A *bâtard* is a large loaf about 3 inches in diameter. A *baguette* is thinner, about 2 inches in diameter and very long; this dough will make 4 *baguettes.* A *ficelle* is a very thin, crisp loaf, about 1 inch in diameter; this dough will make 6 to 8 *ficelles.*

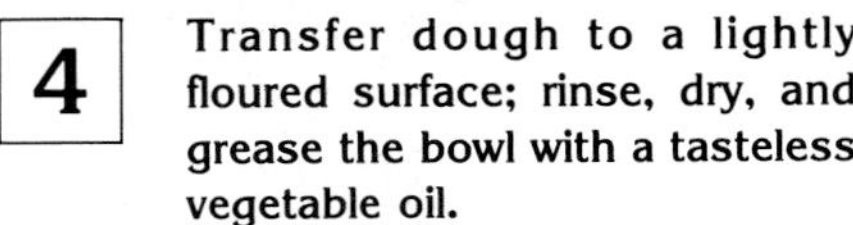

4 Transfer dough to a lightly floured surface; rinse, dry, and grease the bowl with a tasteless vegetable oil.

5 Knead dough for 8 to 10 minutes, until it is smooth and elastic, adding a bit more flour if necessary.

6 Let dough rest for a minute or two, then knead it again briefly.

10 Turn dough out on a lightly floured surface, punch it down, and divide it into 2 or 4 equal-size portions.

11 Using the palms of your hands, roll each piece out to about 17 inches for bâtards, or longer and thinner for baguettes.

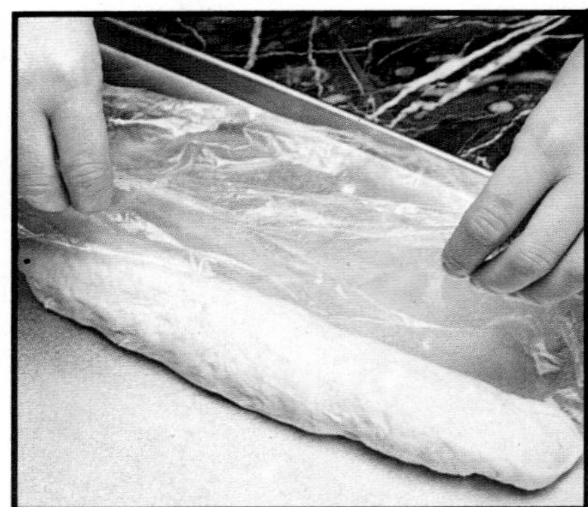

12 Place each loaf on a lightly oiled baking sheet, cover, and let rise until doubled, 30 to 45 minutes.

1 Crumble fresh yeast into warm water (80° to 90°F), or dissolve dry yeast and sugar in warm water (110° to 115°F).

2 Place flour and salt in a large bowl. Make a well in the center and pour the foamy yeast mixture into it.

3 Use a round-bladed knife or wooden spoon to draw the flour into the liquid until fully incorporated.

7 Form dough into a ball and place in the oiled bowl. Cover with a towel or oiled plastic and let rise for 45 minutes to 1 hour.

8 Turn dough out on a lightly floured surface and punch it down. Knead briefly and form into a ball.

9 Return dough to the bowl, cover, and let it rise again for 30 to 45 minutes.

13 Preheat oven to 425°F. With a long sharp knife, make diagonal slashes at 2-inch intervals on the tops of the loaves.

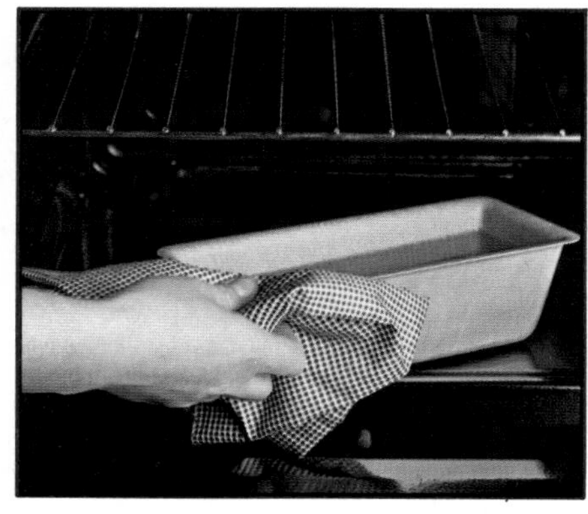

14 Place a pan of hot water on the oven floor and place the baking sheet just above the center level of the oven.

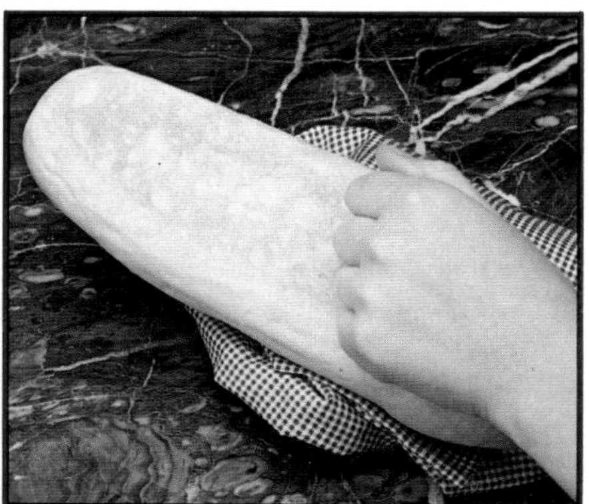

15 Bake for 25 to 30 minutes, until the loaves are evenly brown and sound hollow when tapped with the knuckles.

them, or beer, tomato juice, etc. The liquid should be at the same temperature as the water or milk in which the yeast was dissolved. This is the "comfort" the living yeast needs in order to grow.

Milk increases the nutritional value of the bread and helps a bit in preserving freshness.

The warm temperature of the liquid is essential in bread making *except* when using the food processor. The speed of the motor tends to heat the dough. If the liquid were warm, the dough would become overheated and rise too rapidly, resulting in a loss of texture. Therefore, when making bread with the processor, the yeast is dissolved in *warm* water but the additional liquid used should be *ice cold.* You will find that the kneaded dough is warm, not hot, and the rising time will be of normal length.

Use the metal blade of the food processor if your model does not have a special plastic dough-kneading blade or hook.

Since humidity varies and flour absorbs moisture from the air, you will find that the amount of liquid you add will vary, depending on the humidity.

Salt

Salt not only brings out flavor, it is a part of the baking process as it helps make the gluten firm and helps control the action of the yeast.

Shortening

Shortening, whether butter, margarine or oil, softens the gluten, which improves elasticity and results in increased rising of the dough. It also adds flavor and helps bread to retain freshness.

Sugar

Apart from the small amount used to activate the yeast, sugar is not a necessary ingredient in bread doughs and is used merely as a flavoring agent.

Equipment

You will need measuring cups of varied sizes, from 1/4 cup to 1 cup. These are

Many Ways to Shape a Loaf

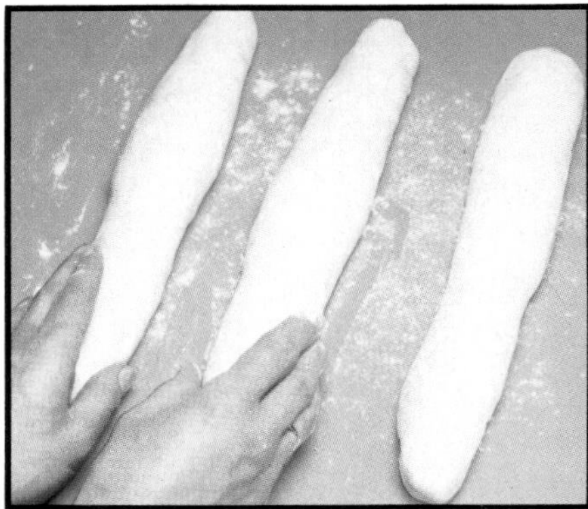

1 *Three-stranded braid:* **Place 3 strands of dough parallel on a working surface.**

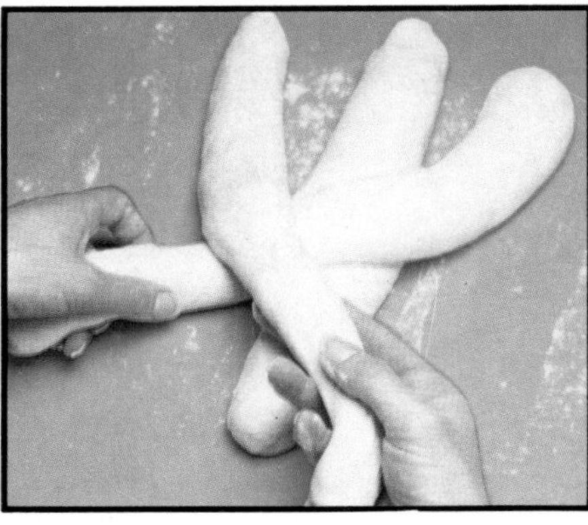

2 **Begin at the center: cross right-hand strand over the center, then the left-hand strand over the right-hand and center strips.**

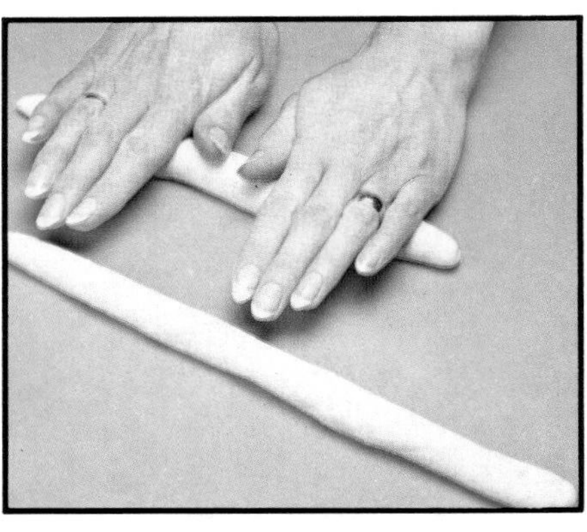

1 *Five-stranded braid:* **Divide dough into 5 equal pieces. Roll each into a long strand. Make a 3-stranded braid.**

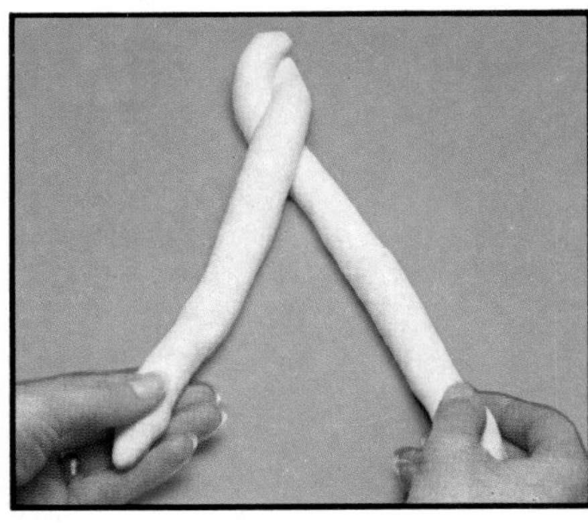

2 **Cross remaining 2 strands and secure ends. Hold one strand in each hand.**

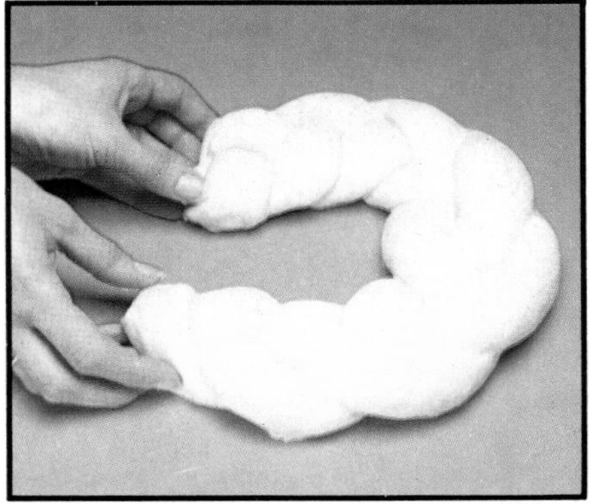

1 *Horseshoe:* **Use a braided loaf, and bring the ends together to shape a horseshoe.**

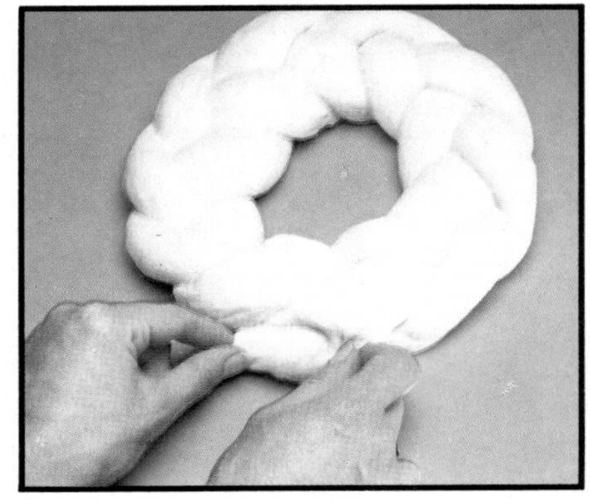

1 *Wreath:* **Make a braided loaf but do not secure the ends. Bring ends around to a circle; weave ends together to secure them.**

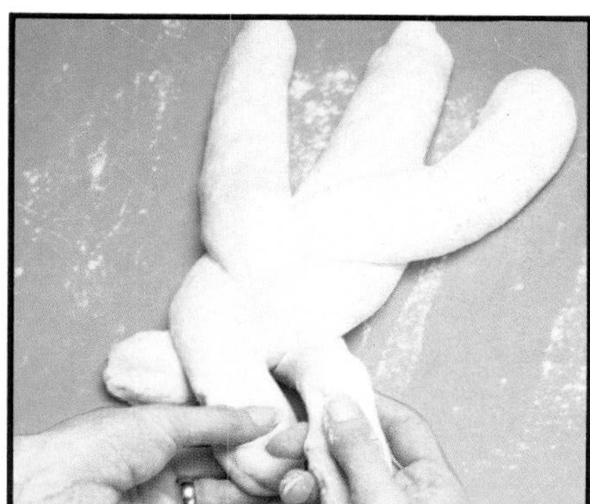

3 Continue braiding the 3 strands of dough until you reach the end. Pinch ends together to seal.

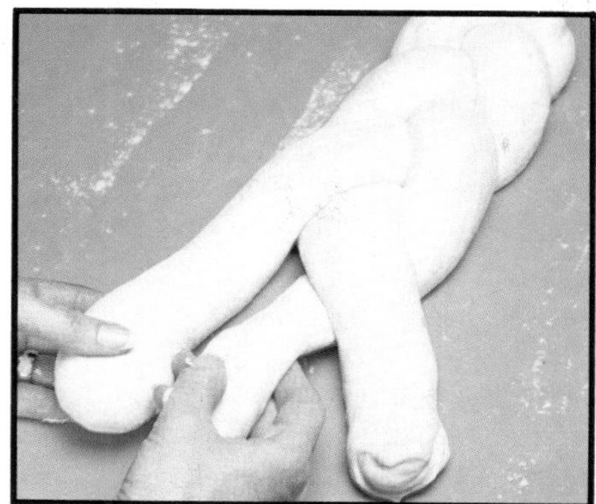

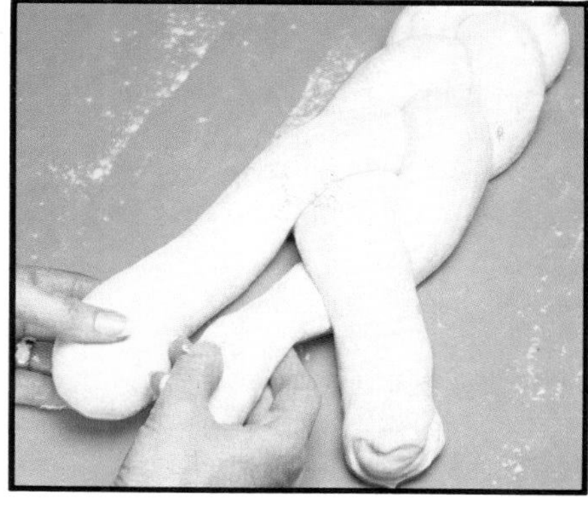

4 Turn dough over with unbraided strands toward you and braid those in the same fashion. Pinch ends together to seal.

3 Pass one strand over the other. Change hands; continue crossing strands until you reach end. Pinch ends to secure them.

4 Place the 2-stranded twist on top of the 3-stranded braid. Transfer the loaf to a baking sheet.

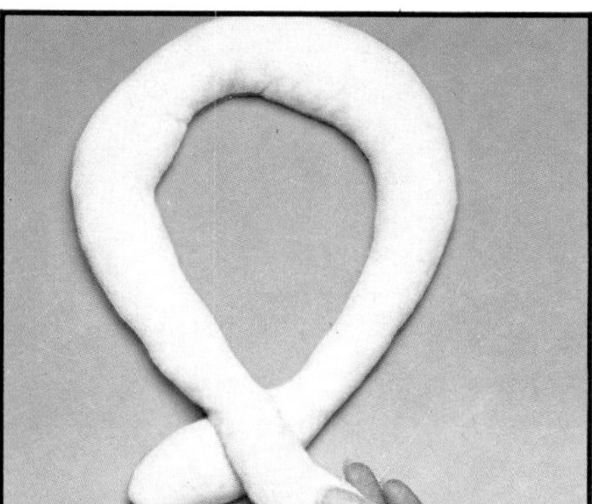

1 *Twist:* Make a long sausage of the dough. Bring the ends together, making a loop with the ends crossed.

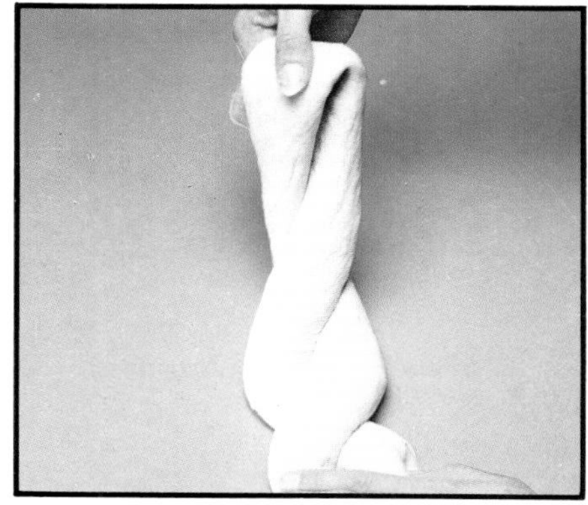

2 Put index finger in the loop while holding the crossed ends. Twist the index finger and dough loop until dough is twisted. Secure.

made of metal or plastic and are called "dry" measures. You should also have measuring spoons. A glass measuring cup, or "liquid" measure, is also needed. A dough scraper is a help in bread making. This is a rectangular metal piece, about 4 × 5 inches, with straight edges and either a wooden or metal handle.

Bread dough can be formed and baked on an ordinary baking sheet. For the conventional loaf shape, a pan 9×5×3 inches is the size for a loaf weighing about 1 ½ pounds; the recipe will use 4 cups of flour.

A size 8½ × 4½ × 2¾ is suitable for a recipe using 3 cups of flour.

The pan can be metal or clay and should always be lightly greased before baking. Dark pans absorb heat and make a crisper crust. The black steel pans can rust so be sure they are thoroughly dried if you wash them after baking. Many cooks do not wash bread pans but store them with their slight protective grease coating.

Bread can also be baked in round pans or coffee cans. The dough should half-fill the pan. If there is too much dough for the size of the pan, the dough can overflow the pan or the loaf may not cook through.

A pastry brush is used to glaze a loaf. With some delicate doughs, such as brioches, a goose-feather glazing brush is appropriate. Glazes can be melted butter, milk, egg yolk, egg white, or salt and water. Nuts or seeds (caraway, poppy or sesame seeds) are often sprinkled on the top of the loaf after glazing.

Making the Bread

There are two basic methods of making yeast bread. In the first method the dissolved yeast is combined with the flour, salt, additional liquid, and shortening if used. The dough is then kneaded and placed in a bowl to rise. In the second method the dissolved yeast is combined with liquid and *part* of the flour. This mixture is allowed to rest until it becomes frothy and bubbly, which will take from 20 to 25 minutes.

This is called a "sponge." The rest of the flour, and eggs if used, are added and the dough is kneaded and placed in a bowl to rise.

Kneading

Dough is kneaded to insure a good rise and to give texture to the bread. When the yeast is added to the flour it softens the gluten. Kneading offsets this softening. It stretches and strengthens the gluten, interlocking the gluten strands, thus helping to form a firm structure to hold in the gas bubbles that the yeast produces until the dough is set by baking.

Kneading is a simple process of stretching and pushing the dough. This is done by hand or with the dough hook of an electric mixer or in a food processor until the dough feels firm and elastic. When sufficiently kneaded, the dough should no longer feel soft or stick to your fingers. If you have added too much liquid the dough will remain soft and sticky. This can be remedied by kneading in a little more flour until the dough feels smooth, not sticky.

Kneading by Hand. Place the dough on a lightly floured surface and very lightly flour your hands. Keeping your fingers together, fold the dough toward you. Then push down and away with the heels of both hands, stretching out the dough. Now fold it toward you again, so that it is compact. Give the dough a quarter turn so that it will be stretched in a different direction. Repeat the process. You should develop a rocking action as you knead and turn. Continue to knead for 10 minutes.

Kneading with a Dough Hook. If you have a mixer with a special dough hook attachment, follow the manufacturer's directions. One usually puts the yeast and liquid in the work bowl, gradually adds the flour at low speed, and then kneads at a moderate speed for about 8 minutes.

Kneading with a Food Processor. The speed of a food processor is such that the dough is completely kneaded in 1 minute. The flour and salt are placed in the work bowl and the machine is run for just a few seconds to mix them. Shortening, if used, is added next and processed to cut it in. The dissolved yeast is poured through the feed tube and the additional liquid (which should be ice cold) is added. Run the machine until the dough forms a ball, at which point start timing for the 1-minute kneading.

Rising

After the dough is kneaded, it is formed into a ball and set aside, covered, to rise. Place it in a well-greased bowl, turn it so that the entire surface is greased, and cover it with a piece of lightly greased plastic wrap. It can also be placed in a well-greased plastic bag, large enough to allow the dough to double, tightly closed.

White bread rises faster than whole-meal bread and all doughs rise faster in a warm place. Dough will even rise in a refrigerator, but that will take hours, compared with 45 minutes for white bread dough in a warm place. The slower the rise, the better the texture of the finished loaf. If for any reason you must interrupt the rising process, place the dough in the refrigerator or freezer. This will slow down or stop the rising but not hurt the dough. When dough is returned to room temperature, the rising will continue.

To test if the rise is complete, gently push a fingertip into the dough. If the resulting indentation fills up shortly, the dough is still rising. If the indentation remains, the dough is risen.

Single and Double Rises. Traditional bread-making methods called for the dough to have 2 rises in the bowl before being formed into a loaf for the final rise. A double rise in the bowl does improve texture. but a single rise plus the final rise in the pan produces a very fine loaf.

When making a brioche dough there must be 2 lengthy rises before forming the brioche for the final rise in the brioche mold or molds.

Punching Down. After the dough is risen completely, it is "punched down" to deflate it and expel the air bubbles created by the gases from the yeast. Punching down is done with clenched fists. Press down with your knuckles all over the dough to flatten it completely and remove all air bubbles. Knead the dough briefly, let it rest for a few minutes, and then form it into a loaf. If the dough is to have 2 rises before shaping, you can punch it down in the bowl and knead it briefly before covering it again for the second rise.

Pat or roll out the dough into a rectangle. For a loaf pan, one side of the rectangle should be the length of the pan. Roll the dough tightly, tuck the ends under and place it, seam side down, in a greased pan. Cover the pan and let the dough rise again before placing it in a preheated oven.

Overrisen Bread. If, for one reason or another, the dough has been allowed to rise too long, it will collapse completely when it encounters the oven heat. Therefore, if this has happened, punch the dough down and let it rise again before baking.

You can test for overrisen bread with your fingertips. Press gently on the top of the loaf. If the loaf starts to deflate it is overrisen. If the indentation of your fingertip remains, but the dough does not deflate, it is completely risen. If the indentation of your fingertip starts to fill up and disappear, the dough is still rising.

Whole-meal loaves will do better if they are placed in the oven just before they are completely risen. You will quickly learn the feel of a risen loaf and the varying times of rising, depending on the composition of the dough and the room temperature. Remember also that bread dough is very "tolerant." It is not as delicate as a cake batter, which must be baked immediately. With bread, you can retard the rising by placing the dough in a cold room or in a refrigerator or freezer, and the finished loaf will be just as delicious.

Special Baking Tips

If you wish your bread to have a crusty finish, it is necessary to introduce steam. Place a container of water in the

More Ways to Shape a Loaf

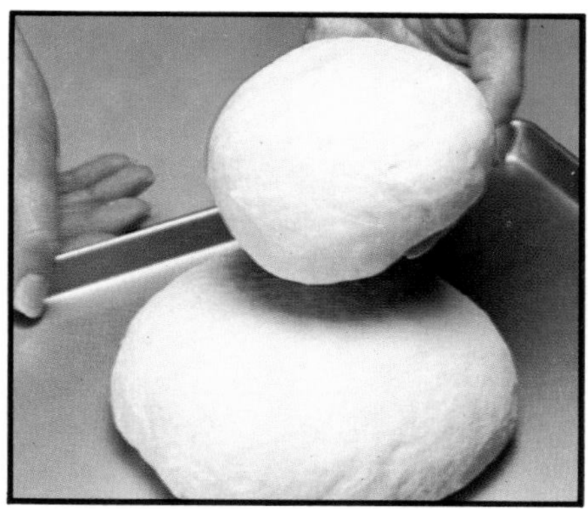

1 *Cottage loaf:* Divide dough into 2 pieces, one twice as large as the other. Shape into balls. Place larger on prepared baking sheet.

2 Place the small ball on top of the large one. Press the floured handle of a wooden spoon down through both balls to join them.

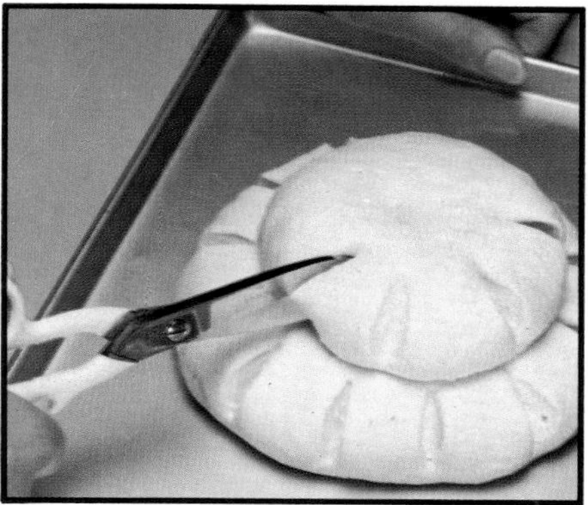

3 Using kitchen scissors, notch the sides of both large and small balls by snipping with the tips of the blades.

1 *Round rolls:* Using the palm of one hand, roll 2 ounces of dough into a ball shape, using a circular motion.

2 Press down, then ease up the hand to cup fingers around the ball, still using a circular motion.

3 Continue to roll the dough until a perfect ball shape is produced. A whirl mark will show underneath.

1 *French bread shape:* Shape a fat sausage about 17 inches long. Slash the loaf 5 times across the width with a sharp knife.

1 *Round loaf:* Shape dough into a ball, place on a baking sheet, and flatten with the palm of the hand. Cut a cross in the top.

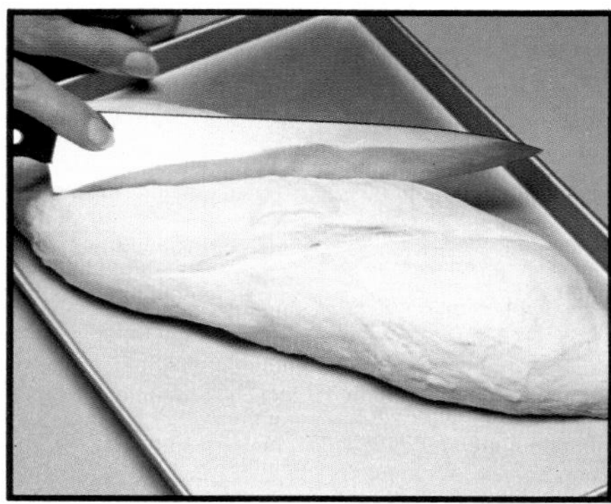

1 *Bâton:* Shape the dough like a French bread, only thinner, with more pointed ends. Slash twice on the diagonal.

Forming Large and Small Brioches

1 Brush the mold with melted butter and form three quarters of the dough into a ball. Place in the buttered mold.

2 Make a hole in the center of the dough. Form remaining piece of dough into a ball shape with a tail. Insert the small ball, tail down, in the hole of the larger piece.

OR Divide dough among individual brioche molds, using three quarters of the dough. Make small balls for topknots, as for a large brioche.

3 Brush tops of brioches with egg wash, being careful not to let it drip down the sides. Let rise until tripled, about 1½ hours. Brush gently with egg wash after rising.

bottom of the oven; as the water evaporates in the oven, the steam it gives off helps the bread to rise and give a crusty top. Another method is to paint the bread surface with water, or spray it with water from a plant sprayer.

Loaves should be placed in the center of preheated 375°F oven and baked for 30 to 35 minutes depending on size of loaves. Rolls need 10 to 20 minutes. When the crust is golden brown, turn loaf out and tap on bottom. If it sounds hollow, it is done. If loaves test done, set them on racks to cool.

Shapes of Loaves

Loaves can be baked in a standard loaf pan or in a round cake pan. The dough can be formed into a free-form round or oval loaf. Dough can be rolled with your hands into a sausage shape and formed into a ring. It can be formed into balls that are placed, touching each other, in a ring mold.

An appealing-looking loaf is made by dividing the dough into 20 pieces. In a long narrow pan or standard loaf pan, make 2 rows, with 7 balls of dough in each row. The 2 rows should touch each other. Place the remaining 6 balls of dough on top along the center between the 2 rows.

Flavored Breads

After mastering basic bread-making techniques you may want to bake flavored breads for some occasions. The flavorings can be either sweet or savory. In some cases the flavoring ingredient is added to the flour in the initial kneading process. In others, such as when adding onions, the flavoring is added after the first rise at the time of shaping the dough for baking.

Cheese gives a delicious flavor to bread and also increases its food value. When adding cheese, usually a hard cheese or mixture of hard cheeses, it should be finely grated so that it will be evenly distributed in the dough. Allow 4 to 6 ounces (1 to 1½ cups) for 4 cups of flour.

Other flavorings, such as ground nuts, chopped fresh herbs or dried spices, are also added at the beginning of the bread-making process. A nice touch when making cheese bread is to add tomato purée to the liquid. This gives an interesting color and a complementary flavor with the cheese.

For a sweet flavor, add dried fruits such as raisins, currants or dates. Candied citrus peel can be added to the dried fruits. These flavorings should be added after the dough has risen for the first time. The fruit should be cut into very small cubes or bits and kneaded into the risen dough. From 4 to 6 ounces of fruit is sufficient for 4 cups of flour. If you are using grated fresh lemon or orange rind, 2 tablespoons is sufficient for 4 cups of flour.

Honey Oatmeal Bread

2 loaves

- **1 envelope active dry yeast, 1 scant tablespoon**
- **1 teaspoon sugar**
- **¼ cup warm water, 105° to 115°F**
- **1 cup oatmeal (see Note)**
- **1¼ cups boiling water**
- **½ cup milk**
- **4 tablespoons butter**
- **2 to 3 teaspoons salt**
- **¼ cup honey**
- **1½ cups whole-wheat flour**
- **3 cups unbleached flour**

Dissolve yeast and sugar in warm water. Place oatmeal in a bowl and pour the boiling water over it; stir. Scald the milk by bringing it to a boil and immediately removing it from the heat. Add the butter to the scalded milk, stir until butter is melted, and add the mixture to the oatmeal. Add the salt and honey, stirring well. When the mixture is lukewarm, stir in the yeast mixture. Combine the 2 flours and add gradually, 1 cup at a time, until dough is firm enough to knead. Knead on a lightly floured surface until smooth and elastic; add more flour if dough is sticky. Place the kneaded dough in a well-buttered bowl, cover with buttered plastic wrap or a towel, and let rise until doubled, about 1 hour.

When dough is risen, remove from the bowl and knead briefly. Divide into 2 equal pieces. Form dough into loaves and place each loaf in a buttered 6-cup pan, 8 × 4 inches. Cover the pans. Let loaves rise for about 45 minutes, until doubled. Preheat oven to 375°F.

Bake the loaves for about 40 minutes, until they are brown on top. Cool in the pans for about 10 minutes, then remove from pans and cool on a rack.

Note: This is regular old-fashioned oatmeal, not instant oatmeal.

Anadama Bread

Legend has it that Anadama bread was invented by a poorly fed husband, finally out of patience with his wife, who muttered to himself as he threw it in the oven, "Anna, damn her."

2 loaves

- **½ cup corn meal**
- **1 cup boiling water**
- **1 envelope active dry yeast, 1 scant tablespoon**
- **¼ cup warm water, 105° to 115°F**
- **¼ cup molasses**
- **2 teaspoons salt**
- **2 tablespoons butter, softened**
- **4½ cups unbleached flour**
- **butter for bowl and pans**

Place corn meal in a large bowl and pour in the boiling water. Stir thoroughly and let cool to lukewarm. Dissolve the yeast in the ¼ cup warm water and set aside until foamy. Add the molasses, salt and butter to the corn meal and stir in the dissolved yeast. Beat thoroughly, gradually adding the unbleached flour. Turn dough out on a lightly floured board and use a spatula or a dough scraper to start kneading. Use only enough additional flour to make it possible to handle the sticky dough. Knead briefly, shape into a ball, and place in a well-buttered bowl. Set dough aside, covered, to rise until doubled, 1 to 1½ hours.

When dough is risen, punch it down and form into 2 equal rectangles. Roll up each rectangle to make a loaf and fit each one into a buttered 6-cup loaf pan, 8 × 4 inches. Cover and let rise again until doubled. Preheat oven to 375°F.

Bake the loaves for about 45 minutes, until they sound hollow when rapped with the knuckles. Cool on a rack.

White Bread

2 loaves, 1 pound each

- 2 envelopes active dry yeast, 2 scant tablespoons
- 1 cup warm water, 110° to 115°F
- ½ to 1 teaspoon sugar
- 1½ cups milk
- 6 cups all-purpose flour
- 2 to 3 tablespoons salt
- 4 ounces butter or margarine, softened
- 3 teaspoons softened butter, for bowl and pans
- 1 egg (optional)
- 1 tablespoon cream or milk (optional)

Dissolve the yeast in the warm water and stir in the sugar. Mix thoroughly and set aside until the mixture foams, about 5 minutes. Scald the milk by bringing it just to the boil. Turn off immediately and cool to 110° to 115°F. Place the flour in a large bowl, add the salt, and stir lightly. Add the 4 ounces softened butter or margarine, the scalded milk and the yeast mixture. Mix well until the flour has absorbed all the liquid. Turn the dough out on a lightly floured work surface. With lightly floured hands, knead dough until it is smooth and elastic, about 10 minutes. During the kneading, add more flour if necessary to prevent sticking. Shape the dough into a ball and place it in a bowl coated with 1 teaspoon of the butter. Roll the ball of dough around to coat the entire surface with butter. Cover the bowl with a towel or a lightly buttered sheet of plastic wrap and set it aside in a warm, draft-free place until the dough has doubled in bulk, from 45 minutes to 1 hour, or more depending on the room temperature.

When dough has risen, punch it down and knead it in the bowl for 2 minutes. Cover the bowl and let it rise again, about 30 minutes or so, which will greatly improve the texture. If time does not permit, you can remove the dough from the bowl after the first rising, and proceed with the recipe.

Divide the dough into halves, roll or pat out each half to a flat layer, and form it into a loaf. Place the loaves in two 6-cup loaf pans, each coated with 1 teaspoon butter. Cover with a towel or buttered sheet of plastic wrap and set pans in a warm place until dough has risen, about 30 minutes. The center of the loaf should be level with the top of the pan. Preheat oven to 375°F.

For a professional-looking glaze, beat 1 egg with 1 tablespoon of cream or milk. Use a pastry brush to paint this mixture on the tops of the loaves.

Bake the bread in the middle of the preheated oven for about 45 minutes. Test for doneness by rapping the bottom of the loaf with your knuckles. It should sound hollow. If not, bake a little longer. For a crisper crust, some bakers remove the loaf from the pan after 35 minutes and let it bake on the oven rack without a pan.

Turn the finished loaf out of the pan and let it cool completely on a rack before wrapping it.

This recipe can be halved.

San Francisco Sourdough

2 loaves

Sourdough Starter

- 1 cup all-purpose or bread flour
- 2 tablespoons sugar
- 1 cup milk

Sponge

- 1 cup starter, at room temperature
- 5 cups all-purpose or bread flour
- 3 cups warm water, 105° to 115°F
- 2 tablespoons sugar
- 2 tablespoons salt

Dough

- ¾ teaspoon baking soda
- 2 tablespoons vegetable oil
- 6 cups all-purpose or bread flour
- 1 teaspoon unsalted butter for baking sheet

To make the starter, mix flour, sugar and milk in a 1-quart screw-top jar; seal tightly. Ferment for 3 to 5 days. Open the jar daily to allow gas to escape; stir down the starter. When the mixture is bubbly and sour-smelling, it is ready.

Make the sponge a day before making the bread. In a large mixing bowl, stir together the starter, flour, water, sugar and salt. Leave in a warm place, covered with plastic wrap, until the sponge has doubled, 24 to 36 hours.

To make the dough, stir down the sponge; sprinkle baking soda over the top and add the oil. Stir to mix thoroughly. Gradually add 6 cups of flour, a little at a time, to make a stiff dough. Turn dough out on a lightly floured surface and knead until dough is smooth and elastic, about 10 minutes. Occasionally throw the dough down hard on the work surface. Cut dough into 2 pieces; let them rest, covered, for 5 minutes. Shape the dough into round balls and place them on a buttered baking sheet. Let loaves rise in a warm place until almost doubled, about 1 hour. Preheat oven to 400°F and position oven rack in the center.

Place a pan of hot water on the lower rack of the oven. Brush the tops of the loaves with water. With a very sharp knife or a razor blade, slash a deep cross in the top of each loaf. Bake loaves until well browned and bottoms sound hollow when tapped with the knuckles, about 45 minutes. Cool loaves slightly on a wire rack. Serve them warm.

Potato Bread

2 loaves

- 1 envelope active dry yeast, 1 scant tablespoon
- 2 tablespoons sugar
- ½ cup lukewarm potato cooking water
- 4 ounces butter, softened
- 2 eggs
- 1 tablespoon salt
- 1 cup mashed cooked potatoes
- 1 cup warm milk, 105° to 115°F
- 6 cups unbleached flour
- melted butter for glaze (optional)

Dissolve yeast and sugar in the warm potato water. Cream the butter and beat in the eggs, one at a time. Add the salt and mashed potatoes and beat well. Add the yeast mixture and stir in the milk. Gradually add the flour, until the dough is stiff enough to knead. Add more flour, if necessary. Knead the dough until smooth and elastic, about 10 minutes. Place in a buttered large bowl, cover, and let rise for about 1 hour, until doubled in bulk.

Turn dough out on a lightly floured work surface and knead it for about 2 minutes. Divide into 2 equal portions and form each into a loaf shape. Place each loaf in a well-buttered loaf pan, 9 × 5 inches. Cover with a buttered sheet of plastic wrap and let rise until doubled, about 45 minutes. Preheat oven to 375°F.

Bake the loaves on the middle level of the oven for 40 to 45 minutes, until loaves sound hollow when rapped on the bottom. Cool on a rack.

For a shinier crust, brush the tops with melted butter before baking.

Raisin Nut Bread

2 loaves

- 1 cup boiling water
- 1 cup milk
- 4 tablespoons butter
- 2 tablespoons sugar
- 2 teaspoons salt
- 1 envelope active dry yeast, 1 scant tablespoon
- ½ cup warm water, 105° to 115°F
- 6 cups unbleached flour
- ¾ cup raisins
- ¾ cup chopped walnuts

Pour the boiling water and the milk into a large bowl. Stir in the butter, sugar and salt. Cool to lukewarm. Dissolve the yeast in the ½ cup warm water and add to the bowl. Gradually add the flour, 1 cup at a time, stirring it in. Turn the dough out on a lightly floured surface and knead for a few minutes. Let the dough rest for about 10 minutes. Knead the dough again, working in the raisins and nuts. Continue to knead until dough is smooth and elastic. Form into a ball and place in a well-buttered bowl, turning the dough to coat all sides with butter. Cover and let rise until doubled, about 1 hour.

Punch dough down, form into 2 loaves, and place in buttered 6-cup loaf pans, 8 × 4 inches. Cover and let rise again until doubled. Preheat oven to 375°F.

Bake the loaves in the oven for 45 to 50 minutes. Cool them on a rack.

Cuban Bread

2 long loaves

- 1 envelope active dry yeast, 1 scant tablespoon
- 2 teaspoons sugar
- 2 cups warm water, 105° to 115°F
- 1½ tablespoons salt
- 6 to 7 cups unbleached flour
- 2 tablespoons corn meal

Dissolve the yeast and sugar in the warm water in a large bowl. Beat in the salt and flour, 1 cup at a time, beating after each addition. Stir in as much of the flour as you can with a wooden spoon, and knead in the rest. Knead on a lightly floured surface for about 5 minutes, then place in a well-buttered bowl and cover with buttered plastic wrap or a towel. Let rise until doubled, 1 to 1½ hours.

When dough has risen, remove it to a lightly floured work surface, knead very briefly, and divide into 2 equal parts. Form each part into a tapered oval loaf, about 15 inches long. Place loaves on a baking sheet that has been sprinkled with corn meal. Cover and let rise for about 5 minutes. Slash the tops diagonally with a very sharp knife. Place the baking sheet with the 2 loaves in the upper part of the *cold* oven. Place a small pan of boiling water on the floor of the oven.

Turn oven control to 400°F. Bake loaves for 20 minutes. Remove loaves from the oven and brush tops with cold water. Return to the oven for about 25 minutes more. The crust should be crisp and brown. Cool loaves on a rack.

Whole-Wheat Bread

2 loaves

- 2 envelopes active dry yeast, 2 scant tablespoons
- 1½ tablespoons sugar
- 1½ cups warm water, 105° to 115°F
- 4 cups whole-wheat flour
- 2 cups unbleached flour
- 1 tablespoon salt
- ¾ cup warm milk, 105° to 115°F
- 3 tablespoons melted butter
- ½ cup honey
- butter for bowl and pans

In a large bowl, dissolve the yeast and the sugar in ½ cup of the warm water. Combine the flours and the salt and add to the yeast mixture, then add the rest of the water. Combine the warm milk with the melted butter and the honey and add this mixture to the flour; mix well. Turn dough out on a floured work surface. Knead until smooth and elastic, about 10 minutes. Form into a ball and place in a well-buttered bowl. Cover with plastic wrap or a towel and let rise until doubled, 1½ to 2 hours.

Punch dough down, divide into 2 equal portions, and form each part into a loaf. Place the loaves in well-buttered 6-cup loaf pans, 8 × 4 inches. Cover and let rise until doubled. Preheat oven to 375°F.

Bake the loaves for about 35 minutes. Remove loaves from the pans and bake directly on the oven rack for about 10 minutes longer, until loaves sound hollow when rapped with knuckles. Cool loaves on a rack.

Swedish Rye Bread

2 loaves

- **2 envelopes active dry yeast, 2 scant tablespoons**
- **1 teaspoon plus 2 tablespoons brown sugar**
- **2½ cups warm milk, 105° to 115°F**
- **4 cups rye flour**
- **4 cups stone-ground whole-wheat flour**
- **2 teaspoons salt**
- **1 tablespoon caraway seeds**
- **flour or corn meal for baking sheet**
- **melted butter**

Pour ½ cup of the milk into a pitcher or bowl and dissolve the yeast and 1 teaspoon of the sugar in the milk. When foamy, pour in the rest of the milk. Combine the flours with the salt and 2 tablespoons brown sugar in a large bowl. Make a well in the center and pour the milk and yeast mixture into the well. With a wooden spoon, draw the flour into the liquid and stir until all the flour is incorporated. Turn the dough out on a floured surface. With floured hands, knead dough until it becomes smooth and elastic. It will be a sticky dough, and you may have to add more flour to knead it. Form dough into a ball and place in a well-buttered bowl. Cover with buttered plastic wrap or a towel. Let dough rise until doubled, about 1½ hours.

Punch down the dough, turn it out on a floured surface, and knead for several minutes, adding the caraway seeds to the dough as you knead. Divide the dough into 2 equal pieces and form each one into a round loaf. Alternatively, place each half in a well-buttered 8-inch round cake pan. If you are making free-form loaves, set them on a baking sheet that has been sprinkled with flour or corn meal. Set the loaves aside, covered, until they have risen and are almost doubled in bulk. Preheat oven to 400°F.

Bake the loaves for 45 to 50 minutes, until they sound hollow when rapped with the knuckles. Brush loaves with melted butter and cool on a rack.

Finnish Rye Bread

1 oval loaf

- 1½ envelopes active dry yeast, scant 1½ tablespoons
- 1½ cups warm milk, 105° to 115°F
- 4¼ cups unbleached flour
- 1 cup rye flour
- 2 teaspoons salt
- flour or corn meal for baking sheet

Dissolve the yeast in the warm milk in a large bowl until foamy. Combine the flours and mix in the salt. Gradually add the flours to the milk and yeast. Dough will be sticky. Add enough more flour so that you can knead the dough. Knead it on a lightly floured board for about 10 minutes. Form dough into a ball and place in a well-buttered bowl. Cover and let rise until doubled in bulk.

When dough is risen, punch it down and form into an oval loaf. Sprinkle a baking sheet with a little flour or corn meal and place the loaf on it, covered, to rise until almost doubled. Preheat oven to 400°F.

Pierce the loaf at random with a fork. Place in the oven. After about 10 minutes, turn oven heat down to 350°F and bake the loaf for about 30 minutes more. Cool it wrapped in a towel.

Tangy Mustard Bread

1 loaf

- 2 envelopes active dry yeast, 2 scant tablespoons
- 1 teaspoon sugar
- ½ cup warm water, 105° to 115°F
- 2 cups unbleached all-purpose flour
- ⅔ cup whole-wheat flour
- ⅔ cup rye flour
- 1 teaspoon salt
- 2 tablespoons butter, softened
- ½ cup prepared strong mustard, such as Dijon-style mustard
- 3 to 4 tablespoons warm water
- butter or margarine for coating bowl and pan
- 1 egg white (optional)

Dissolve the yeast and sugar in the warm water; stir well, and set aside until the mixture foams. Place the flours and the salt in a large bowl and mix together well. Work in the butter and the mustard until evenly distributed. Add the yeast mixture and stir it in well. Add as much of the additional warm water as needed. Turn dough out on a lightly floured surface and knead it for about 10 minutes. The dough will be sticky because of the rye flour. Form dough into a ball and place in a buttered bowl, turning the dough to coat the entire surface with butter. Cover and let rise in a warm place until doubled in bulk, about 1½ hours.

Punch dough down, knead briefly, and return it to the bowl to rise for the second time, about 1 hour.

When risen, pat or roll the dough into a rectangle. Roll it up, tuck the ends under, and place in a well-buttered 6-cup loaf pan. Cover and let rise until doubled, 45 minutes to 1 hour. Preheat oven to 375°F.

Beat egg white with 1 tablespoon water if you wish to glaze the loaf. Brush the loaf with the egg-white mixture. Bake on the middle level of the oven for about 40 minutes. Remove loaf from the pan and cool on a rack.

Poppy-Seed Twist

1 large loaf

- 2 packages active dry yeast, 2 scant tablespoons
- 1 cup warm water, 110° to 115°F
- 4 teaspoons sugar
- 5 to 6 cups all-purpose flour
- 2 teaspoons salt
- 3 whole eggs, beaten
- 4 tablespoons unsalted butter, softened
- 1 egg yolk
- 2 tablespoons milk
- ¼ cup poppy seeds

Dissolve the yeast in the warm water with ½ teaspoon of the sugar; set aside. Place 5 cups of the flour in a large bowl. Add the salt, eggs, remaining sugar and the butter; blend well. When the yeast mixture is foamy, pour it into the flour mixture. Stir well until all the liquid has been absorbed. Turn dough out on a lightly floured surface. Knead it for 8 to 10 minutes, adding more of the flour if necessary. Form dough into a ball and place in a buttered bowl. Turn the ball of dough so it is buttered on the entire surface. Cover the bowl with a towel or buttered sheet of plastic wrap and let it rise until doubled, about 1 hour.

When dough is risen, punch it down with your fists and let it rise a second time, covered.

When risen again, punch the dough down and divide it into 3 or 5 equal portions. With the palms of your hands, roll out the portions of dough to make ropes of equal length, and braid them as shown in the illustrations for Three-Stranded or Five-Stranded Braid. Place the braided loaf on a lightly buttered baking sheet. Tuck ends under the loaf, cover with a towel or buttered sheet of plastic wrap, and let rise for about 30 minutes. Preheat oven to 375°F.

Beat egg yolk with 2 tablespoons milk to make a glaze. Brush the entire loaf with the glaze and sprinkle with the poppy seeds. Bake in the middle of the oven for about 30 minutes, or until the bread is a shiny deep brown. Remove from the oven and place on a rack to cool.

Refrigerator Dough

(Processor Method)

1¾ pounds dough

- **1 envelope active dry yeast, 1 scant tablespoon**
- **1½ tablespoons sugar**
- **¼ cup warm water, 105° to 115°F**
- **3¼ cups unbleached flour**
- **4 tablespoons unsalted butter, at room temperature**
- **2 tablespoons solid vegetable shortening, at room temperature**
- **1 teaspoon salt**
- **2 large eggs**
- **⅓ cup cold milk**

Dissolve the yeast and the sugar in the warm water, and let stand at room temperature for 5 to 10 minutes. Use a food processor fitted with the steel blade to process the flour, butter, shortening and salt for 20 seconds. With the machine running, pour the eggs and the yeast mixture through the feed tube. Then pour in the milk in a steady stream as fast as the flour mixture will absorb it. Process for 30 seconds. Scrape the dough into a well-buttered 3-quart mixing bowl. Cover tightly with a sheet of oiled plastic wrap and refrigerate until the dough has doubled in bulk, 4 to 6 hours.

Punch down the dough. If you do not use it immediately, cover it tightly and refrigerate for up to 4 days. Punch down the dough just before using it.

Variation: This enriched dough can be used for coffeecakes, braided breads, small buns or sweet rolls. Add nuts, raisins or citrus fruits.

Mozzarella Wheat Bread

1 large oval loaf

For the bread

- **2 envelopes active dry yeast, 2 scant tablespoons**
- **2 teaspoons sugar**
- **1½ cups warm water, 105° to 115°F**
- **3 cups whole-wheat flour**
- **1 cup cracked wheat (see Note)**
- **1½ cups unbleached flour**
- **1 tablespoon salt**
- **1 teaspoon freshly ground black pepper**
- **¼ cup olive oil**
- **flour or corn meal for baking sheet**

For the filling and topping

- **8 ounces mozzarella cheese**
- **4 tablespoons butter, softened**
- **15 pitted black olives**
- **½ teaspoon dried marjoram**
- **1 teaspoon minced fresh basil**
- **12 to 14 anchovies**

Dissolve the yeast and sugar in ½ cup of the warm water. Combine the whole-wheat flour with the cracked wheat, half of the unbleached flour, and the salt and pepper. Mix well, and blend in the olive oil. Add the dissolved yeast and the rest of the warm water and stir to blend. Turn the dough out on a lightly floured surface and knead until it is smooth and elastic. Form into a ball and place in a well-buttered bowl. Cover and let rise until doubled, 1½ to 2 hours.

Punch down the dough and form it into a large oval loaf. Place on a baking sheet that has been sprinkled with flour or corn meal and let rise, covered, for about 1 hour. Preheat oven to 400°F.

Bake the loaf for about 20 minutes. Reduce oven heat to 350°F and bake for about 30 minutes longer, until the loaf sounds hollow when rapped with the knuckles. Place on a rack to cool completely before slicing and filling. Cool overnight if possible.

Preheat oven to 425°F. Cut the cheese into thin slices. Let the butter soften to room temperature. Halve the olives. Slice the completely cooled bread, making ½-inch slices and cutting almost but not quite through to the bottom. Insert the slices of mozzarella between the slices of bread. Combine the softened butter with the marjoram and basil and spread the mixture on the top of the bread. Place the anchovies over the top in a diagonal crisscross. Decorate with the olive halves. Place the loaf on a lightly oiled baking sheet and bake for about 15 minutes. Serve immediately.

Note: Cracked wheat, sometimes called bulgur, is sold in health-food stores as well as ethnic grocery stores, and in many supermarkets. It comes in 3 grades; the medium or coarse wheat should be soaked in boiling water for about 10 minutes and drained before being added to the flour. Rye meal, if available, can be used instead of cracked wheat.

Gannat

(Cheese Bread)

2 loaves

- **1 envelope active dry yeast, 1 scant tablespoon**
- **½ teaspoon sugar**
- **¼ cup warm water, 105° to 115°F**
- **8 ounces butter, softened**
- **8 eggs**
- **1 to 1½ teaspoons salt**
- **4 to 5 cups unbleached flour**
- **6 ounces Gruyère cheese, grated (1½ cups)**

Dissolve the yeast and sugar in the warm water; stir, and set aside until foamy. Cream the softened butter and add the eggs, one at a time; mix well. Add the salt. Stir in the yeast mixture. Gradually stir in the flour until the dough is stiff enough to knead. You may not need all 5 cups of flour; the dough should be soft. Add the grated cheese. Turn dough out on a lightly floured surface and knead for about 5 minutes. Place dough in a buttered large bowl and turn it to coat the entire surface with butter. Cover the bowl with a piece of buttered plastic wrap or with a towel. Set dough aside to rise until doubled in bulk, 1 to 1½ hours.

When dough is risen, turn it out on a lightly floured surface. Knead it briefly, then divide it into 2 pieces; form each piece into a loaf. Place each loaf in a buttered loaf pan or a buttered 9-inch round cake pan. Let dough rise again, covered with plastic or a towel, until doubled, about 1 hour. Preheat oven to 400°F.

Bake the loaves on the middle level of the oven for 30 to 35 minutes, until loaves are an even brown and sound hollow when rapped with your knuckles. Remove loaves from the pans to cool on a rack.

Other cheeses used may be Swiss Emmenthaler or a sharp Cheddar.

Brioche

makes 1¼ pounds dough

12 individual brioches or 1 large brioche

1 envelope active dry yeast, 1 scant tablespoon
¼ cup plus pinch of sugar
¼ cup warm milk, 110° to 115°F
2 cups all-purpose flour
¾ teaspoon salt
3 eggs, beaten
6 ounces unsalted butter, softened but cold
1 egg, for egg wash
melted butter for molds

Dissolve the yeast and the pinch of sugar in the warm milk in a small bowl. When the mixture is foamy, add ½ cup of the flour; blend the sponge thoroughly with a wooden spoon. Transfer the mixture to a large bowl, scatter 1½ cups flour over the sponge, and cover with a buttered sheet of plastic wrap or a towel. Let rise for 1 hour.

With a wooden spoon, or the flat paddle of an electric mixer, beat ¼ cup sugar, the salt and the eggs into the sponge. Add the butter, 3 or 4 tablespoons at a time, until well incorporated. If using a mixer, be careful not to overmix. Cover the dough and let it rise for about 3 hours, until tripled in bulk.

Stir the dough down, cover the bowl, and place it in the refrigerator. After 1½ hours, stir down again. Cover and refrigerate overnight. The dough will keep in the refrigerator for 2 to 3 days, or in the freezer for 1 week. If frozen, thaw the dough in the refrigerator overnight.

Beat the egg for the egg wash. Brush ⅓-cup molds or a large brioche mold with melted butter. Form the brioches and brush the tops carefully with the egg wash. Let dough rise again until tripled, about 1½ hours. Brush carefully with egg wash again. Preheat oven to 375°F.

Bake the brioches on the middle level of the oven, 17 minutes for individual brioches, 30 to 40 minutes for a large brioche or a loaf. The tops should be a shiny dark brown.

Food Processor Brioche

makes ¾ pound dough

9 individual brioches, or 1 small loaf

- **1 teaspoon active dry yeast**
- **2 tablespoons plus a pinch of sugar**
- **2 tablespoons warm milk, 110° to 115°F**
- **1¼ cups all-purpose flour**
- **2 eggs**
- **½ teaspoon salt**
- **7 tablespoons butter**
- **1 egg, for egg wash**

Dissolve the yeast and the pinch of sugar in the warm milk in a small bowl. Scrape the mixture into the work bowl of a food processor fitted with the steel blade. Add ¼ cup of the flour and 1 egg. Process very briefly, just enough to combine the ingredients. Sprinkle remaining flour over the sponge mixture. Cover and let rise in the work bowl for 1½ to 2 hours.

Add 2 tablespoons sugar, the salt and the second egg. Process for about 15 seconds. Add the butter by tablespoons through the feed tube while the motor is running. Do this very quickly and process for 30 to 40 seconds. Sprinkle the top of the dough with a tiny bit of additional flour. Cover and let rise until tripled in bulk, about 3 hours.

Stir the dough down and refrigerate the work bowl containing the dough for about 20 minutes. Turn the dough out on a lightly floured surface. With floured hands, pat it out into a rectangle about 9 × 5 inches. Fold the dough in thirds, as for a business letter. Dust very lightly with flour and refrigerate the dough, wrapped in plastic, overnight.

The next day, brush ⅓-cup brioche molds or a loaf pan with melted butter, and form the brioches. Beat the egg for egg wash and brush it over the brioches. Let the dough rise for 1½ to 2 hours. Brush with egg wash again. Preheat oven to 375°F.

Bake the brioches on the middle level of the oven for about 17 minutes for individual ones, or for 30 minutes for a small loaf or large brioche.

Walnut Fruit Bread

1 loaf, 2 pounds

- **1 envelope active dry yeast, 1 scant tablespoon**
- **¾ cup warm water, 105° to 115°F**
- **3 cups all-purpose flour**
- **1 cup whole-wheat flour**
- **2 tablespoons sugar**
- **1 teaspoon salt**
- **½ cup warm milk, 105° to 115°F**
- **¾ cup sour cream**
- **1⅓ cups seedless raisins**
- **½ cup chopped walnuts**
- **⅓ cup chopped dried apricots**
- **butter for bowl and loaf pan**

Dissolve the yeast in ¼ cup of the warm water in a bowl and set in a warm place until foamy, about 10 minutes. Sift flours, sugar and salt into a large mixing bowl. Make a well in the center and pour the milk into the well, along with remaining ½ cup water, the yeast liquid and the sour cream. Gradually stir flour into liquid until it is all incorporated and the dough comes away from the sides of the bowl. Turn dough out on a lightly floured surface. Knead until smooth and elastic, 8 to 10 minutes. Add more flour if necessary to prevent sticking. Place dough in a buttered large bowl and turn dough to coat all sides with butter. Cover the bowl with a damp cloth and set it in a warm, draft-free place until the dough has doubled in bulk.

Turn dough out on the floured work surface and knead for 5 minutes. Roll dough into an oblong. Sprinkle with the raisins, walnuts and apricots. Knead fruits and nuts into the dough and shape it into a large loaf. Place the dough in a buttered loaf pan. Cover the pan with a damp cloth and set it in a warm place until dough has risen to the top of the pan, about 30 minutes. Preheat oven to 400°F and position the oven rack in the center.

Bake the bread for 45 to 50 minutes, until it sounds hollow when the bottom is tapped with the knuckles. Cool on a wire rack.

Part Four

ICES AND ICE CREAM

I scream,
You scream,
We all scream
For ice cream!
—street song

Ice cream has come to be considered an all-American food, like apple pie, hot dogs and hamburgers, and small surprise that this is so, since Americans consume an incredible 14.5 gallons each per year. Nevertheless its origins are definitely in Europe, where it had achieved a fairly wide popularity nearly 100 years before it was available, to a privileged few, in America. No one knows exactly when or where ice cream was invented, although the term "ice cream" was supposedly coined by a visitor to the governor's mansion in Maryland in 1744.

Fruit-flavored ices have been made since very early times. Ices like the French *sorbet* and Italian *granita* were made long ago by Arabs, who called them *sherbets,* and drank them. The Chinese made flavored water ices, as did the Indians and Persians. The Romans were known to enjoy a dish of snow flavored with honey.

Catherine de Médicis brought with her entourage a cook who took the French court by storm with his elaborate iced desserts, but according to Theodora Fitzgibbon, " 'Cream ices' were popularised by Tortoni, owner of a Paris café in the late 18th century, when it became the fashion to serve a *bombe glacée* at the end of a formal meal in France. Water ices, or *sorbets,* used to be served between courses during a meal, to refresh and clear the palate for the next course . . ." *(The Food of the Western World)*

For many years ice cream remained a popular, although expensive, treat for wealthy Europeans. Once exposed to ice cream, the average

American took to it with a vengeance, so that by 1837 an English visitor was most astonished to see "common laborers" enjoying it.

The history of ice cream is inextricably bound up with mankind's ability to harvest, transport and store ice, for it was not until the end of the nineteenth century that ice was made artificially, and not until the 1920s and 1930s that home refrigeration became at all common. Before that ice was big business, and fortunes were made harvesting it and selling it.

Laura Ingalls Wilder provides an excellent description of how ice cream was made at home:

" 'Let's make ice-cream!' Royal shouted.

"Eliza Jane loved ice cream. She hesitated, and said, 'Well—' Almanzo ran after Royal to the ice-house. They dug a block of ice out of the sawdust and put it in a grain sack. They laid the sack on the back of the porch and pounded it with hatchets till the ice was crushed. Alice came out to watch them while she whipped egg-whites on a platter. She beat them with a fork, till they were too stiff to slip when she tilted the platter.

"Eliza Jane measured milk and cream, and dipped sugar from the barrel in the pantry. It was not common maple sugar, but white sugar bought from the store . . .

"She made a big milk-pail full of yellow custard. They set the pail in a tub and packed the snowy crushed ice around it, with salt, and they covered it with a blanket. Every few minutes they took off the blanket and uncovered the pail, and stirred the freezing ice-cream." *(Farmer Boy)*

In 1846 a woman named Harriet Johnson invented a hand-cranked, household ice-cream freezer. She never patented the device, but it was destined, nevertheless, to make ice cream a staple in nearly every American home. Shortly thereafter, commercially produced ice cream began to be available and by the 1870s ice-cream parlors were flourishing in towns all over America.

Several people have claimed the distinction of vending the first ice-cream cone, and the conflicting claims may never be sorted out. Everyone seems to agree that it happened at the St. Louis World's Fair of 1904, and records indicate that a total of 5,000 gallons of ice cream was sold each day.

From that point on the record gets a bit clearer. A Danish immigrant named Christian Nelson came up with the first chocolate-covered ice cream bar in 1919. Three years later it was marketed as an Eskimo Pie and a million of them were sold on a single day. The first ice cream on a stick? It was the Good Humor Ice Cream Sucker, invented by a man named Harry Burt in the 1920s, and it was sold, then as now, by Good Humor men in clean white trucks with ringing bells.

As refrigeration came into more common use, the commercial manufacturing of ice cream increased proportionately. According to John F. Mariani, ". . . ice cream took on a positively sanitary image in the 1940s, and Hollywood movies pictured ice cream soda fountains as oases of innocent Americana. In World War II newspapers printed photos and stories of GI's and sailors who missed nothing back home so much as ice cream." *(The Dictionary of American Food & Drink)*

As the home-cranked freezer fell into disuse and people turned increasingly to the commercially manufactured product, the quality of American ice cream declined. Much of the ice cream produced today is inflated with air to give it bulk, filled with additives and artificial flavors, fortified with emulsifiers to make it stiff enough to hold the air, and finally treated with stabilizers to prevent the formation of ice crystals.

Unquestionably, homemade ice cream, with simple pure ingredients, far surpasses any product you can buy. Today, with a refrigerator in every home, and a freezer compartment in every refrigerator, making ices and ice creams is child's play indeed. Very good ice cream and sherbet can be made with no more complicated equipment than a shallow metal tray and the freezer compartment of your refrigerator. If you object to having crunchy crystals within the texture of your sherbet or ice cream, you merely have to stir the mixture a few times while it is freezing. Otherwise just leave it until it's done.

For those who feel that hand-churned ice

cream is still the ultimate ideal, a large variety of electric ice-cream freezers is available on the market, to do all the work for you. With one of these at hand you need only decide upon the flavor and the richness you want, for you can make everything from the lightest, low-calorie, to the very richest, extra-dense, custard-enriched, high-butterfat ice cream.

According to one statistic there exist today 300 flavors of ice cream; who knows—a clever and resourceful ice-cream fanatic may be able to set new records right at home.

ICES AND ICE CREAM

Despite the mystique that surrounds ice-cream making, there are no special techniques or equipment needed, and anyone who can follow a recipe can make ices that are superior to any commercial product.

The simplest point at which to start is with ices—granitas, water ices and sorbets, elegant combinations of sugar syrup, flavoring and sometimes egg white, frostily tangy and impressive to serve to guests.

Once you are familiar with ices, move on to ice cream. There are 3 basic types of ice cream, each of which is made by a different method. The first two—simple fruit ice cream and cream ices—are the quickest and easiest. Custard-based ice cream, the basis of the classic vanilla ice cream, is a little more time-consuming but should present no problems if you follow the step-by-step instructions.

All you need to make these frozen desserts is a freezer, some ice-cube trays or a bread pan, and an electric mixer or rotary egg beater; plus patience of course, because they do take time. The results, however, are worth waiting for.

Ices

There are three basic types of ice.

Granita. This is the easiest of all to make, being simply a weak sugar syrup flavored with tea, coffee or fruit juice. A granita is a cross between a drink and an ice and is perfect as a cooling summer refresher.

Traditionally, a granita is served in a tall glass, topped with cream. A long spoon is provided so the top portion can be eaten. The bottom portion is usually drunk.

Water Ice. This is made from stronger sugar syrup flavored with fruit juice or purée. After initial partial freezing, a small amount of egg white is beaten into the ice. It is then frozen again until firm, then beaten again, to break up the ice crystals. After a final freezing, the ice is ready to use. A water ice is generally served as a light dessert.

Sorbet. This is the finest of ices, made from fruit purée or juice added to a very strong sugar syrup. After this stage the same method as that used for water ices is followed, except that a larger quantity of egg white is beaten in to give the finished ice a smooth, light texture. What we know as sherbet often includes milk or gelatin as well.

In old cookery books you may see sorbets referred to as sherbets. They were traditionally served as a refresher in the middle of a large banquet. Today sorbets are usually served as a dessert or as a cooling snack, though fine restaurants, especially French ones, still

Coffee or Tea Granita

4 portions

6 tablespoons superfine sugar
4 ounces roast coffee beans, coarsely ground, or 2 ounces strong tea leaves
whipped cream
coffee beans (optional)

1 Pour 4 cups water into a pan. Add sugar and stir once. Bring to a boil over moderate heat, stirring.

5 Repeat this procedure twice more at 30-minute intervals, until a granular slush is formed.

6 Turn into tall glasses and top with a whirl of whipped cream. Decorate coffee ice with coffee beans and serve.

sometimes serve a sorbet between the first courses and the entrée.

Ice Cream

There are three types of ice cream.

Simple Fruit Ice Cream. This is the simplest to make and is also one of the most popular. A fruit purée is made and whipped cream is folded into it. The biggest advantage of this type is that little or no cooking is required.

Cream Ice. This type of ice cream uses a sorbet as its base. Fruit purée or juice is added to a very strong sugar syrup. This is then frozen and beaten in turns. For a sorbet, the ice is finished by beating in egg white to make a firm snow, which is then frozen. For a cream ice, egg white is not added, but is replaced by lightly whipped cream. The mixture is then frozen.

Rich Ice Cream. This is the most time-consuming ice cream to make and the most expensive, but it gives the most delicious results. A custard is made with cream and eggs. There is a wide choice of flavorings. Chopped nuts and fruits are added after the ice cream has been partly frozen. Alternatively, the ice cream may be combined with puréed fruit, producing a result similar to a cream ice but richer.

Equipment

Freezer. A freezer is the ideal place in which to make ice or ice

2 **Boil for 3 minutes, then remove from heat. Stir in ground coffee or tea leaves and leave for 15 minutes.**

3 **Strain infusion into a jug. Cool, then chill. Pour into ice-cube trays or a loaf pan.**

4 **Cover and freeze for 30 minutes. Turn into a bowl and stir. Cover, return to freezer trays, and re-freeze.**

OR ***Ice-cream maker method:*** **Pack the freezer with layers of ice and rock salt, following manufacturer's instructions.**

Ɛ **Pour the mixture of syrup and coffee infusion into the can and churn for about 15 minutes.**

Ɛ **Serve the granita in stemmed glasses, decorated with whipped cream and candied violets.**

cream. The temperature is at a constant low so there is no need for adjustment. Another advantage is that you can make quite a large quantity of ice or ice cream and store it until needed.

Ice-Cream Makers. Ice-cream makers are certainly the easiest to use for freezing. These appliances freeze the ice and stir it constantly so that a smooth result is obtained. And there is no need to beat between freezings. Models range from old-fashioned hand-cranked freezers to modern streamlined machines. The prices vary accordingly. If you use an ice-cream maker, follow the manufacturer's instructions for freezing.

Other Equipment. You will also need a heavy pan for making syrup; a sieve for straining syrup for making fruit purée; a swivel vegetable peeler for peeling citrus rinds; a juice extractor for citrus fruits; a bowl for cooling syrup; an electric mixer for beating the ice and the cream; 2 metal spoons; aluminum foil to cover the ice cream in the freezer; ice-cube trays, with the dividers removed, bread pans or plastic freezing boxes in which to freeze the ice cream.

In addition to these you will need extra items for ices containing cream. You will need 2 more bowls for beating egg yolks and cream. Depending on your choice of method, you may need a second heavy pan for scalding the cream and a double boiler for cooking the custard.

Ice creams are often made in fancy shapes; they are easier to mold than water ices. Gelatin molds of suitable size can be used, while kitchen shops sell special bombe molds that enable you to produce gorgeous desserts rivaling any chef's creation. If you intend to purchase one of these, make a note of the measurements of your frozen food compartment before you do, to be sure that the mold will fit in comfortably.

Ingredients

Sugar. Superfine or confectioners' sugar may be used for ice cream, as for water ices. Cream ices also include a sugar syrup. The proportion of sugar to other ingredients is most important. If too much sugar is used, the ice will not freeze; too little, and the final result will be so hard that you cannot get your spoon into it.

Liquid. The amount of liquid varies according to the type of ice. Granitas have the most liquid and sorbets the least. For most ices, the liquid is water, except in the case of granitas where tea, coffee, or a mixture of cider and water may be substituted. The liquid is always made into a syrup with the sugar and other flavoring.

Cream gives its name to ice cream. Many commercial mixtures called ice cream contain no cream whatsoever, but cream is an essential ingredient of homemade ice cream. Light or heavy cream may be used, according to individual recipes. Heavy cream is needed for simple fruit ice creams and is added toward the end when making certain ices. The cream is usually lightly whipped to give the ice cream a thicker texture. It is important to whip only to the soft-peak stage. Whipped beyond this, it will turn buttery when mixed with the other cold or partly frozen ingredients and this will affect the texture of the finished ice cream. Light cream may be used for making the base of a custard ice cream.

Milk may be substituted for light cream in the custard as an economy or emergency measure, but because it is thinner than cream, it tends to give a granular texture to the final product. Extra egg yolks are usually added to counteract this, so although milk might seem cheaper, the economy is most often canceled out. Use milk only in emergencies.

Eggs. Egg white is added to water ices and sorbets to give a light consistency. Use the whites of large eggs. In water ices only ½ egg white is used for an ice to make 4 portions. This is about 1 tablespoon of egg white. If you do not want to be bothered by halving the egg white, make double the quantity of the ice and use all the white. In sorbets more egg white is added.

Neither simple fruit ice creams

Lemon Water Ice

about 6 portions

3 large lemons
3 cups water
1 cup superfine sugar
egg white from 1 large egg

4 Cool the syrup and strain it. Chill it in the refrigerator.

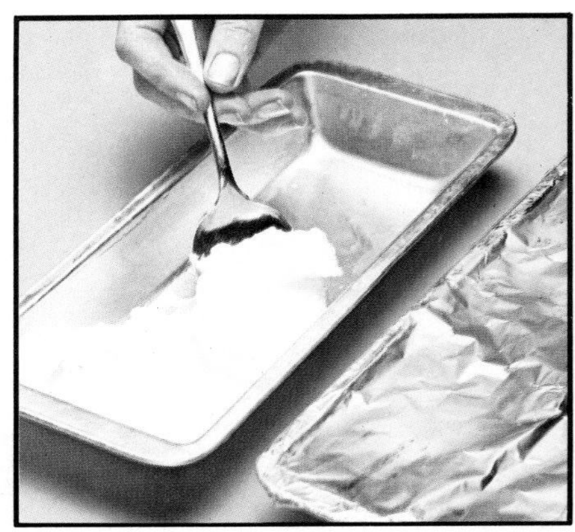

8 When a firm snow is formed, cover ice and return to freezer. Freeze for 1½ hours.

1 Pare the rind from 3 large lemons with a swivel vegetable peeler. Extract the lemon juice.

2 Pour 3 cups water into a pan. Add lemon rind and juice and 1 cup superfine sugar. Stir once.

3 Place over moderate heat and bring to a boil, stirring. Reduce heat and simmer for 5 minutes.

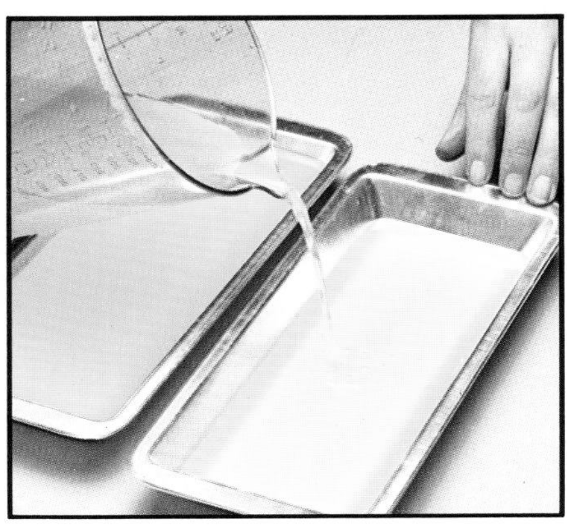

5 Pour the mixture into ice-cube trays or a bowl. Cover and freeze for 30 minutes, until slushy.

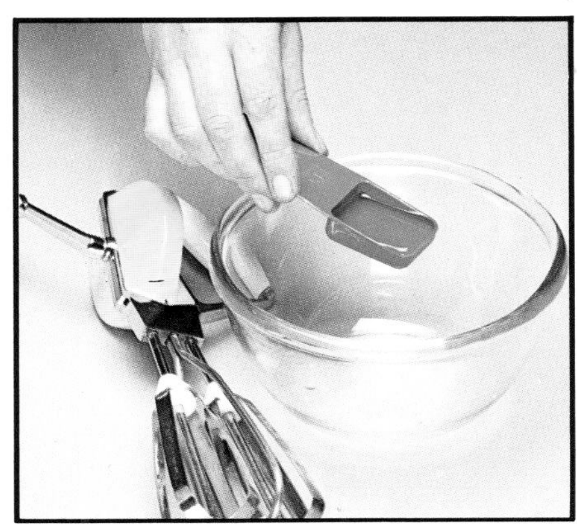

6 Measure out half of 1 large egg white and beat it until it stands in soft peaks.

7 Remove ice from the freezer. Stir, then beat it into the egg white in spoonfuls.

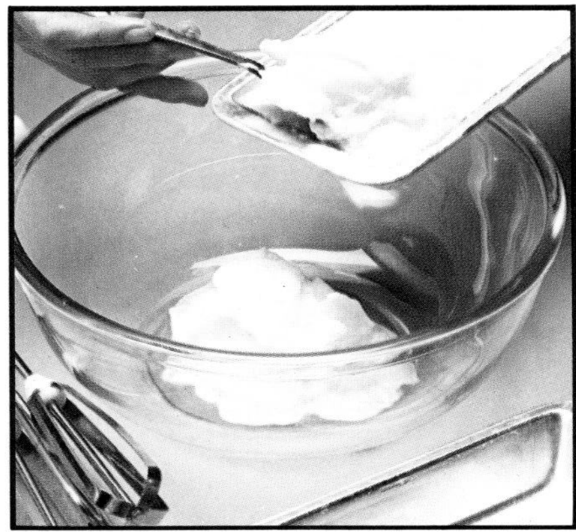

9 Remove ice from freezer, turn into a bowl, and beat again.

10 Put in the freezer tray again, and freeze.

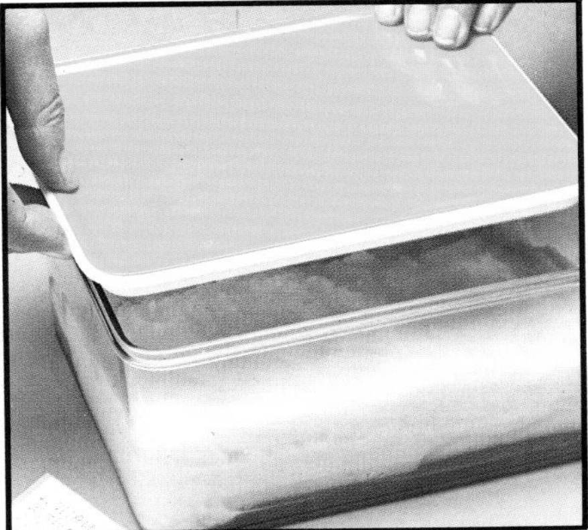

11 Pack in a rigid box for freezer storage. Leave at room temperature for 30 minutes before serving.

Custard-Based Vanilla Ice Cream

4 to 6 portions

1 cup light cream
1 vanilla bean, or 2 or 3 drops of vanilla extract
1 whole egg
2 extra egg yolks
¼ cup superfine sugar
1 cup heavy cream

1 Scald light cream together with vanilla bean. Cover and allow to infuse for 15 minutes.

2 In top pan of a double boiler, beat whole egg, extra yolks and sugar until thick.

4 Cook the mixture over hot, not boiling, water. Stir continuously for about 15 minutes.

5 When custard is thick, remove from heat. Add extract if used. Strain, leave to cool, then chill.

6 Turn into freezer container. Cover with foil and freeze for 45 minutes, or until mushy.

8 Turn ice into a bowl and beat thoroughly. Add cream and stir in. Cover and freeze, about 45 minutes.

9 Remove from freezer and beat thoroughly. Return to freezer container, cover again, and freeze.

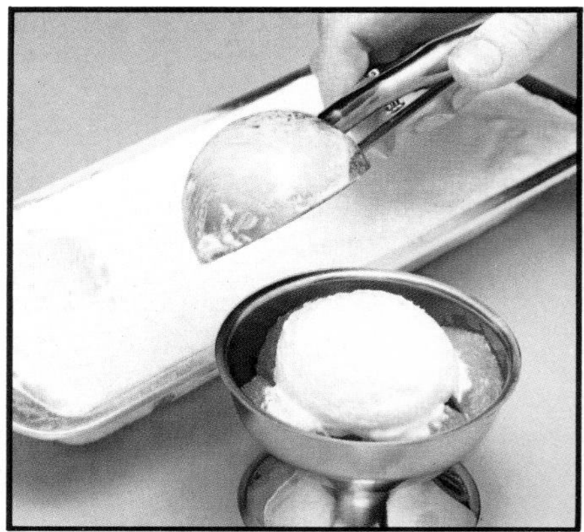

10 Remove ice cream from freezer 20 minutes before serving to allow ice cream to soften slightly.

3 **Pour scalded cream onto beaten eggs in a trickle, stirring continuously.**

7 **Whip the heavy cream to soft peaks; do not let it become stiff.**

Variations: Numerous additions can be made to vanilla ice cream.

To make Chocolate Ice Cream, stir in 1 ounce melted semisweet chocolate of good quality before freezing.

To make Coffee Ice Cream, stir 1 teaspoon instant coffee crystals or 2 tablespoons very strong prepared coffee into the scalded cream.

For Tutti-Frutti Ice Cream, chop 2 ounces glacé cherries, 1 ounce candied angelica and 1 ounce mixed candied orange and lemon rind. Add these with 1 ounce golden raisins soaked in 3 tablespoons Cognac, plus the Cognac.

For Walnut Ice Cream, chop 2 ounces shelled walnuts. Add these with 3 tablespoons Grand Marnier liqueur.

nor cream ices require the addition of egg whites or yolks. But egg yolks are essential to the custard base of rich ice cream. It is the yolks that give vanilla ice cream its golden glow. The richest ice creams are made by using only egg yolks, but whole eggs may be used instead.

Other Additions. Freezing tends to diminish flavor so that all mixtures to be frozen need to be well flavored. Lemon and orange rind and juices and liqueurs are used to enhance fruit ices or may be used alone to flavor ice creams.

Nuts are another addition to ice creams. One famous ice cream, Nesselrode, uses puréed chestnuts; another well-known recipe uses praline, made from caramelized unblanched almonds. Chopped nuts of all kinds give attractive texture to ice creams, as well as adding flavor.

Fruits. Fruity ices are pretty to look at and refreshing on a hot day. In an ice the flavor of the fruit is sharp and fresh after the freezing process. Strongly flavored fruits are best, so choose from apricots, blackberries, black and red currants, grapefruits, lemons, limes, nectarines, oranges, peaches, pineapples, raspberries, strawberries, or tangerines.

For granitas, only the fruits that can be puréed into a juice (blackberries, black and red currants, raspberries, strawberries) and citrus fruit juices are traditionally used. Water ices and sorbets can be made using any of the fruits listed.

Canned fruits may be used, but this is not really worth doing, as one of the joys of homemade ices is the flavor of the fresh fruit. Frozen fruits work well.

When using citrus fruits (oranges, lemons, limes, etc.), the maximum flavor is obtained from the rind by boiling it in the syrup. Pare off the rind in very thin strips with a swivel vegetable peeler. The juice is squeezed from citrus fruits and added to the syrup.

Apricots, nectarines, peaches, pineapple, raspberries and strawberries can all be puréed when raw. All but pineapple can be puréed through a food mill or a sieve. Pineapple can be prepared only in a blender or food processor. All woody parts must be removed first. If you purée fruits containing many seeds in a blender or food processor, the purée must be sieved later to remove the seeds.

Blackberries and currants must be cooked before they can be puréed. Stew them in a little water without sugar. All the sugar in these ices comes from the syrup. The fruit must be drained before being puréed.

Chopped fruits—fresh, canned, glacé or dried—and chopped peels may be added to ice cream. These additions give it a more varied texture. However, it is important that these be added only when the ice cream is near completion, otherwise the extra sugar will upset the balance and the ice cream will not freeze.

Serving and Storing

Granitas must be eaten as soon as they are ready. If kept, they will freeze too far and lose their characteristic granular consistency. Water ices and sorbets may be stored in plastic freezer containers in the freezer for up to 3 months. Before using sorbets or water ices stored this way, leave them at room temperature for about 30 minutes to soften slightly.

Ice cream also may be stored for 3 months. The time needed for softening ice cream will vary with the recipe. Soft-textured ice cream should be removed from the freezer about 15 minutes before serving. Firmer ice cream should usually be removed from the freezer at the start of a meal and put on the bottom shelf of the refrigerator.

The Grand Finale—Bombes, Cassatas and Ice-Cream Cakes

Bombes and cassatas are fancy molded ice creams that reveal their different layers when cut for serving, a delight to the eye. The contrast in textures and flavors inside is also very pleasing.

The outer layer of these domed

desserts is always made of ice cream. A bombe has one hidden layer, which may be made of ice cream, water ice or sorbet; or a special custardlike bombe mixture may fill the center.

A cassata (also the name of a famous Italian dessert) is a 3-layered ice-cream cake, with an outer layer of ice cream, a middle layer of water ice or sorbet, and a center of creamy cassata, a mixture of flavored whipped cream.

Bombes and cassatas are traditionally shaped as a dome in a special mold or small bowl. However, if you find it easier, you can use a round or square cake pan or an oblong bread pan to make an ice-cream cake with a hidden layer in the center rather than the usual horizontal layers. Ice-cream cakes usually have only one inside layer, which can be a contrasting ice cream, a water ice or sorbet, or a bombe or cassata mix.

Equipment

Most of the equipment needed is the same as that for ice and ice-cream making. Depending on your choice of ice cream, you may also need equipment for making special bombe and cassata fillings. For a bombe mixture, these include a heavy pan, sugar thermometer and wooden spoon for making the syrup; a whisk and double boiler for making the custard mixture, and a large bowl and plenty of ice cubes for chilling it. For a cassata center you will need a sifter for the confectioners' sugar and a mixer or rotary beater and bowl for whipping cream. For flavoring you may need a juice extractor and citrus zester, a sieve and spoon for puréeing fruit or a chopping device for chopping fruits and nuts.

The Mold. If you plan to acquire the traditional domed mold, the most useful size to own is 2 cups. Because these frozen desserts are very rich, this will give ample portions for 6 people. All quantities given here are for a mold of this size.

For ice-cream cakes, a loaf pan is the ideal mold as it provides an easy shape to slice for serving. A round cake pan is also attractive.

You will also need some wax paper and scissors. A plastic or rubber spatula is useful for shaping the layers and a thin-bladed metal spatula for leveling the top gives a professional-looking smooth finish to the unmolded dessert.

Making Bombe Mixture

Making this mixture requires time and patience. Allow 1½ hours to make it and cool it sufficiently to the point of being ready to use. A bombe is usually made of 3 parts ice cream to 1 part bombe mixture. Thus, for a 2-cup mold you will need 1½ cups ice cream of your choice and ½ cup bombe mixture.

A bombe mixture made with egg yolks and sugar syrup has a custardlike consistency. The proportions are 2 large egg yolks for every 3 tablespoons superfine sugar and ½ cup water.

Adding Flavorings. This basic bombe mixture can be flavored in various ways, and it can be made lighter by the addition of an egg white beaten stiff, or can be enriched with 2 tablespoons lightly whipped cream. Although the basic mixture can be made ahead, the additions should not be folded or stirred in until just before the mixture is placed inside the mold lined with frozen ice cream.

Here are some suggestions for flavoring ½ cup basic bombe mixture.

- Use 2 tablespoons liqueur such as kirsch, brandy, Cointreau, rum or Drambuie, alone or with a little grated orange rind.
- Add a few raisins that have been soaked in 2 tablespoons sherry for 1 to 2 hours.
- Add 3 tablespoons chopped nuts or praline, or 4 chopped *marrons glacés,* or 2 tablespoons sieved sweetened chestnut purée sprinkled with a drop of rum. Pistachios are traditional and expensive, but worth including for their beautiful color.

Making Cassatas

A cassata is a triple-layered frozen dessert. The proportions used for a 2-cup cassata to make 6 portions are ⅔ cup ice cream, ⅔ cup sorbet or water ice, and a cassata mixture made with 6 tablespoons heavy cream.

You will need to prepare and freeze ahead both an ice cream and a water ice. However, the special cassata mixture that fills the center of the dessert is a good deal quicker and easier to make than the special bombe mixture.

A cassata is made similarly to a bombe. Press the ice-cream lining into the mold; it is not quite so thick as the lining for a bombe and it will take only about 45 minutes to freeze firm. Then press in the sorbet or water-ice layer in exactly the same way; cover and freeze

Bombe Mixture

makes ½ cup

3 tablespoons superfine sugar
2 large egg yolks

optional extras:

flavorings of your choice
2 tablespoons lightly whipped cream
1 large egg white, beaten stiff

Carefully whisk the cooling syrup into egg yolks, adding very little at a time, and whisking between additions.

1 Pour ½ cup cold water into a pan, add sugar, and stir until sugar is dissolved. Bring quickly to a boil.

2 Simmer for 3 minutes, until mixture reaches 217°F. Remove pan from heat and cool in a bowl of water and ice cubes.

3 Beat egg yolks in top pan of a double boiler over hot water until they are thick, light and creamy.

5 When all syrup is added, continue whisking over heat until mixture is doubled in bulk, about 15 minutes.

6 Plunge top pan into ice water. Continue whisking until mixture is thick and completely cold.

7 Fold in flavoring and/or whipped cream or beaten egg white just before you are ready to use the mixture.

again for 45 minutes. When the water-ice layer is frozen, quickly make the cassata mixture, spoon it into the cavity, level it off, cover, and freeze for 1 to 2 hours before unmolding.

Unmolding

Bombes, cassatas and ice-cream cakes are best unmolded the moment they come out of the freezer, while they are still very solid. Fill a bowl with hand-hot water. Wrap the metal mold in a cloth and dip it into the water. Fifteen seconds should be enough time to loosen the ice cream from a metal mold, as metal containers heat quickly. A pottery mold may take as long as 1 minute to warm enough to loosen the ice cream. Invert a plate over the mold, then invert both plate and mold together. Gently lift off the mold.

If a mold is dipped for too long, the surface of the bombe or cassata will melt and need smoothing with a metal spatula. Even if the surface has not melted, perfect its appearance: dip a spatula into boiling water for 45 seconds, dry it, then "polish" the bombe or cassata with a few light smoothing strokes.

Decorating and Serving. Do not serve a bombe or cassata immediately after unmolding but always place it, uncovered, in the refrigerator for about 15 minutes before serving to soften it a little and develop full flavor.

Bombes and cassatas look fine served simply, particularly when cut open to reveal the intricate pattern of their layers. But you can, if you wish, decorate them. Pipe a little cream on the unmolded dessert or top it with frosted fruit.

An alternative to decorations is to pour a few spoonfuls of brandy or liqueur over the dessert just before serving.

Bombes and cassatas are served cut into wedges, like a cake. It is easy to slice them if you use a hot dry knife.

Assembling a Traditional Bombe

6 portions

1 ½ cups ice cream
½ cup Bombe Mixture (see preceding recipe)
flavoring of your choice
1 egg white, beaten (optional)
2 tablespoons lightly whipped cream (optional)
garnish of your choice (optional)

1 Beat ice cream in a bowl until slightly softened and workable, but not runny.

2 Press 2 tablespoons ice cream into a chilled 2-cup mold, spreading it against the base. Hold mold with a cloth.

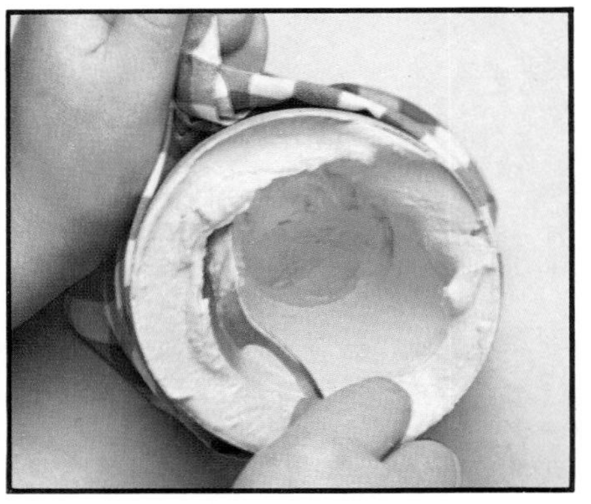

3 Working from base to rim, gradually add more ice cream and line sides of the mold with a layer ½ to 1 inch thick.

4 When lining is firm, smooth and even, cover the mold and set in the freezer for at least 1 hour.

5 Fold flavoring, egg white or cream (if using) into mixture. Spoon into cavity of mold and press down firmly.

6 Fill mold until surface is level. Cover and freeze again for 1 ½ to 2 hours, longer for nonmetal molds.

7 Remove lid, wrap mold in a cloth, and dip it into hot water. Remove cloth. Invert bombe on a plate. Smooth with a spatula.

8 Refrigerate for 15 minutes before serving to soften and develop flavors, then decorate if wished, and serve.

Glace au Café Liégeoise

A variation of the iced coffee served with ice cream in the style of Liège

Glace au Café Liégeoise (continued)

6 portions

For the ice cream

1 cup light cream
1 large egg
2 extra egg yolks
6 tablespoons superfine sugar
3 tablespoons fine-ground coffee
scant ½ cup confectioners' sugar
1 cup heavy cream

For the syrup

½ cup superfine sugar
1 tablespoon instant coffee powder

For the garnish

½ cup whipped cream
grated rind of 1 large orange

4 Cook for 15 minutes, stirring continuously, until thick. Remove from heat and strain into a bowl.

5 Pour ½ cup boiling water over the ground coffee. Leave to infuse. Strain.

6 Mix confectioners' sugar with the strained coffee and stir. Stir mixture into the custard.

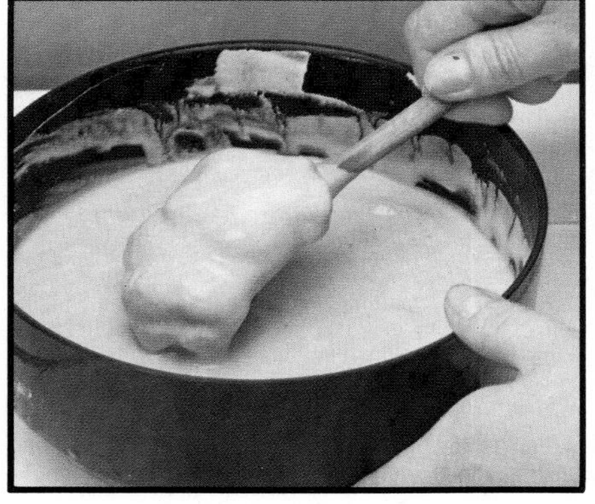

10 Beat ice cream again to break up crystals. Return to container and freeze until required.

11 To make coffee syrup, pour 1 cup water into a heavy pan. Stir in ½ cup superfine sugar.

12 Stir over low heat until sugar is dissolved. Boil, covered, for 15 minutes.

1 Pour light cream into a heavy pan and scald over low heat. Set aside.

2 In top pan of a double boiler beat together whole egg, egg yolks and 6 tablespoons superfine sugar.

3 Set mixture over hot water; stir till mixture is thick. Pour in scalded cream, continuing to stir gently.

7 Pour the coffee custard into a large plastic bowl. Cool, cover, and freeze for 45 minutes.

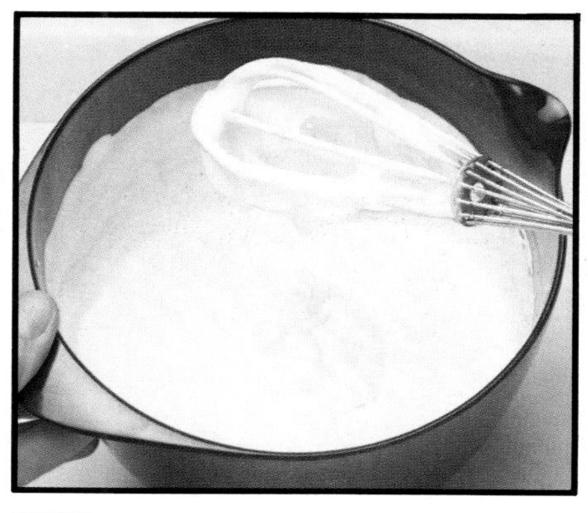

8 Whip heavy cream just until it holds its shape. Remove coffee custard from freezer.

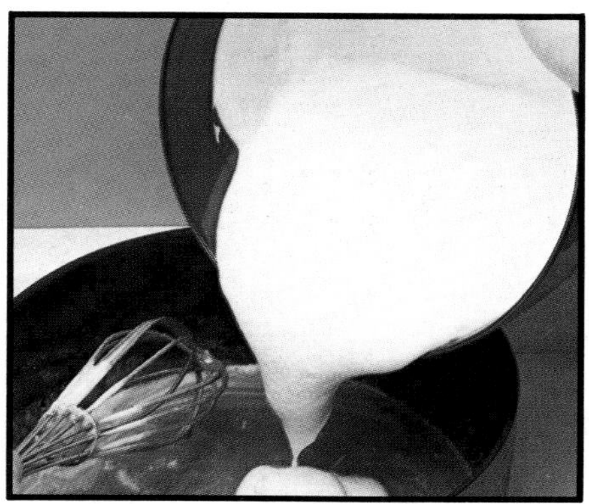

9 Stir coffee custard to break up ice crystals, then beat in the whipped cream. Freeze for 45 minutes.

13 Dissolve instant coffee powder in ¼ cup boiling water. Stir into the syrup. Cool syrup.

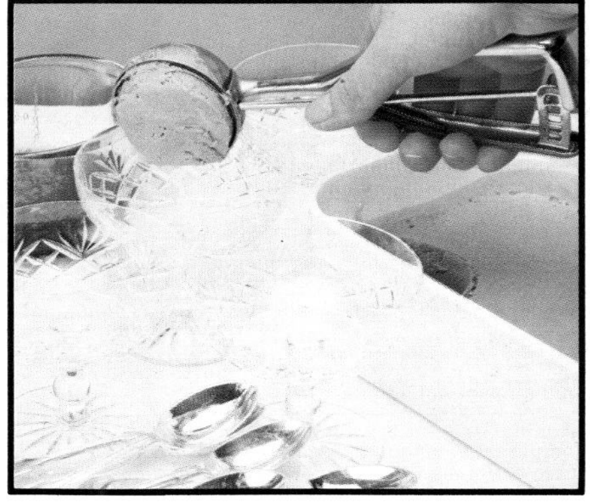

14 To serve, place a generous scoop of coffee ice cream in each dish. Pour a little syrup over each portion.

15 Top with whipped cream, either piped on or spooned on. Sprinkle with grated orange rind.

Apricot Brandy Water Ice

4 portions

1 lemon
1½ cups superfine granulated sugar
½ cup apricot brandy
1 large egg white

Pare the rind from the lemon with a swivel vegetable peeler. Squeeze the lemon juice and set aside. Pour 3 cups water into a heavy pan; add the lemon rind and sugar, and stir once. Set pan over moderate heat and bring to a boil, stirring. Reduce heat and simmer for 5 minutes. Add the lemon juice to the syrup. Cool the syrup, then chill for 10 minutes. Strain the syrup and stir in the apricot brandy. Pour into ice-cube trays or a pan. Cover and freeze for 30 minutes, until slushy.

Measure out half of the egg white and beat it until it stands in soft peaks. Remove ice from the freezer. If it is in ice-cube trays, turn it into a bowl. Stir to break up the ice crystals, then stir the ice into the egg white, a little at a time, using an electric mixer or rotary beater. When a firm snow is formed, cover and return ice to the freezer. Freeze until firm, about 1½ hours.

Remove from the freezer and beat again. Cover and refreeze until firm, about 2 hours. Store the ice in a rigid plastic box in the freezer.

Black-Currant-Leaf Water Ice

4 portions

4 large handfuls of black-currant leaves
3 large lemons
⅞ cup superfine granulated sugar
2 or 3 drops of green food coloring
1 large egg white
4 bunches of black currants

Wash the black-currant leaves in cold water and drain on paper towels or in a salad spinner. Reserve a few of the best leaves for garnish. Pare the rind from the lemons with a swivel vegetable peeler. Squeeze the lemon juice.

Pour 3 cups water into a heavy pan; add the lemon rind and juice, and the sugar; stir once. Set pan over moderate heat and bring to a boil, stirring. Reduce heat and simmer for 5 minutes. Remove from heat and add the black-currant leaves. Stir so they are all soaked in the syrup. Cover the pan and leave to infuse for 30 minutes.

After infusion, strain the syrup, squeezing the leaves to extract all the flavor. Stir in the green coloring. Chill the infusion, then pour it into ice-cube trays or a bowl. Cover and freeze for 30 minutes, until slushy.

Measure out half of the egg white and beat it until it stands in soft peaks. (Refrigerate or freeze remaining egg white for another use.) Remove ice from freezer. If ice-cube trays were used, turn the ice into a bowl. Stir the ice, then beat spoonfuls of the ice into the egg white, using an electric mixer or a rotary beater. When a firm snow is formed, cover the ice and return to the freezer. Freeze until firm, about 1½ hours.

Remove from freezer and beat again. Cover and freeze once more, about 1½ hours. To store, pack ice in a rigid plastic box. Leave at room temperature for 30 minutes before serving. Serve decorated with black-currant leaves and a few berries.

Variations: For Geranium-Leaf Ice, use sweet geranium leaves in the same way. For Mint Ice, use enough mint leaves to fill a 2-cup measure; make the ice in the same way.

Pineapple Sorbet

4 portions

1 medium-size pineapple
2 large egg whites
¾ cup superfine granulated sugar

Cut a slice off the bottom of the pineapple without cutting through to the flesh; the pineapple shell will be used for serving. Cut off the spiky top; keep both shell and top in the refrigerator until ready to serve. Run a knife around the inside of the pineapple shell to loosen the flesh. Hold the fruit upside down so the flesh falls out. Do all this over a plate to catch all the juices. Cut the pineapple into slices. Remove the hard center core and extract the "eyes" with the point of a knife. Chop the pineapple into rough pieces. Place in a blender or food processor and process until pulpy.

Pour 1½ cups water into a heavy pan. Add the sugar and stir once. Set the pan over moderate heat and bring to a boil, stirring. Reduce heat and simmer for 5 minutes. Cool the syrup and strain it into a jug. Chill in the refrigerator.

Mix the pineapple pulp and juice with the syrup. Pour the mixture into ice-cube trays or a bowl. Cover and freeze for 1 hour, until slushy.

Beat the egg whites until they stand in soft peaks. Remove ice from the freezer, and stir it. Beat it into the egg whites, in spoonfuls, with a whisk. When a firm snow is formed, cover the ice and return to the freezer. Freeze until firm, from 1½ to 2 hours. Remove from freezer and beat again for 3 to 4 minutes. Cover and refreeze for about 1 hour.

Pile the sorbet into the cold pineapple shell and replace the spiky top as a lid. Surround with fresh fruit of your choice and mint leaves.

Variations: For Black-Currant Sorbet, simmer 1 pound black currants in water. Drain and purée. Make into a sorbet with 1¼ cups superfine sugar, 2 cups water, 2 tablespoons lemon juice and 2 egg whites. For Raspberry or Strawberry Sorbet, use the same quantities as for black-currant sorbet but reduce the sugar to 1 cup.

Coupe Jacques

(Raspberry and Lemon Sorbet with Fresh Fruit)

6 portions

2 cups assorted fresh fruits
2 tablespoons superfine granulated sugar
2 teaspoons lemon juice
7 tablespoons kirsch
1 pint raspberry sorbet
1 pint lemon water ice
2 ounces blanched almonds, halved (1/3 cup)

Cut the fruits into small pieces. Combine fruits, sugar, lemon juice and 6 tablespoons of the kirsch in a bowl. Mix the fruit well with a spoon. Cover the bowl and chill in the refrigerator for 1 hour.

Rinse 6 large shallow glass bowls (coupes) in cold water. Dry them. Put a large tablespoon of raspberry sorbet and another of lemon sorbet side by side in each bowl, leaving a small space between the 2 mounds of sorbet. Put 2 tablespoons of fruit mixture on top and in between the sorbets. Sprinkle the coupe Jacques with remaining kirsch and decorate with blanched almonds. Serve immediately.

Praline Ice Cream

6 portions

3/4 cup superfine granulated sugar
6 ounces unblanched almonds
1 pint Custard-Based Vanilla Ice Cream (see Index)

Make the praline: Place the sugar in a heavy pan and heat it gently until it melts. Protecting your hand with an oven mitt, stir the sugar with a metal spoon until it turns brown. Quickly stir in the unblanched almonds. Pour the praline onto a sheet of greased aluminum foil or a marble slab. Spread out the mixture to make a thin layer. Let the praline cool.

When praline is cold, break it into pieces and grind them in a mortar with a pestle, or crush them in a bowl with the end of a rolling pin, or grind in a food processor. Mix the praline into the ice cream at the final beating stage, and freeze until firm. (This can also be made with high quality store-bought ice cream. Soften ice cream slightly, beat in praline, and freeze until firm.)

Raspberry and Red-Currant Cream Ice

4 to 6 portions

- **1 cup superfine granulated sugar**
- **2 cups mixed raspberry and red-currant purée**
- **1 lemon or 1 orange**
- **½ cup heavy cream**

Chill the container for the ice cream. Put the sugar in a heavy pan with ½ cup water and stir once. Bring to a boil and boil for 5 minutes without stirring. Cool the syrup. When cold, add it to the fruit purée. Meanwhile, squeeze the lemon or orange. Add the juice to the fruit and syrup. Pour the mixture into the chilled container, cover with a double layer of foil, and freeze for 45 minutes, until the mixture has formed a partly frozen mush.

Whip the cream to the soft-peak stage. Turn the fruit mush into a chilled bowl. Stir briskly to break up any ice crystals, stirring the sides into the middle. Beat in the cream. Return mixture to the freezing container, cover again with foil, and freeze for 45 minutes longer.

Remove the ice from the freezer and beat once more to break up the crystals. Cover again with foil and freeze until firm.

Remove from freezer just before serving as this cream ice is quite soft.

Cassata Napoletana

6 portions

- **⅔ cup Strawberry Ice Cream (see Index)**
- **⅔ cup Black-Currant-Leaf Water Ice (see Index)**
- **1 ounce candied angelica**
- **1 ounce glacé cherries**
- **2 to 3 teaspoons fresh orange juice**
- **6 tablespoons heavy cream**
- **½ teaspoon sifted confectioners' sugar**
- **1½ ounces shelled pistachios or slivered toasted almonds**

Beat the ice cream until it is slightly softened and workable. Line a chilled 2-cup mold with the ice cream. Cover and freeze for 1½ hours if using a pottery mold, for 45 minutes if using a metal mold.

Beat the water ice until softened. Press the ice into the mold to make a second layer. Cover and freeze again for 45 minutes.

Rinse the angelica and cherries under warm water, pat dry with paper towels, and chop fine. Mix with a few teaspoons of orange juice. Whip the cream until it just holds its shape. Fold in the confectioners' sugar, then the angelica, cherries, and pistachios or almonds. Spoon this cassata mixture into the mold lined with ice cream and water ice. Cover and freeze again for 1 to 2 hours, or for 3 hours if using a pottery mold.

Uncover the mold. If it is metal, wrap it in cloth to protect your hands. Dip the mold into a bowl of hand-hot water for 15 seconds, or for 1 minute if you are using a pottery mold. Turn out the cassata on a plate, smooth the surface with a spatula, and refrigerate for 15 minutes before serving.

Variations: For Brazilian Cassata use vanilla ice cream and coffee sorbet. Flavor cassata mixture with 6 tablespoons chopped Brazil nuts and 2 teaspoons rum. Decorate the unmolded bombe with grated chocolate and Brazil nuts.

For Pineapple and Praline Cassata, use praline ice cream and pineapple sorbet. Flavor the cassata mixture with 4 tablespoons raisins, plumped up in rum, and 4 tablespoons crystallized pineapple, rinsed, dried and chopped.

Honeymoon Cassata is made with chocolate ice cream, tangerine sorbet and a cassata mixture flavored with chopped mandarin orange sections and hazelnuts.

Perfect Pink Cassata is made with vanilla ice cream and raspberry and red-currant sorbet. The cassata mixture is flavored with chopped fresh strawberries sprinkled with orange juice and grated orange rind.

Fudge Ripple Molds

6 portions

- **8 ounces dark semisweet chocolate**
- **2 ounces vanilla fudge**
- **1 tablespoon heavy cream**
- **1½ cups vanilla ice cream**

Use three 1-cup plastic yogurt, sour cream or cottage cheese containers as molds. Wash them thoroughly and dry well. Chill the containers.

Melt the chocolate in a bowl placed on a trivet in a pan of gently simmering water. Spoon about ¼ cup of the melted chocolate into one of the well-chilled containers. Swirl it around so the sides and base are evenly coated. Pour any surplus back into the bowl of chocolate. Coat remaining molds in the same way. Cover the molds and place in the freezer for about 10 minutes.

Meanwhile melt the fudge and the cream in a pan over very low heat. Beat the ice cream to soften it a little, then stir the fudge mixture through it to give a ripple effect. Divide the ice cream among the chocolate-lined molds, level tops, and cover with wax paper and foil. Freeze for about 45 minutes. This is enough time for small molds.

To unmold, uncover, and cut the containers into halves with a sharp knife, slicing through the ice cream at the same time. Remove the container halves. Place each half mold flat side down on a plate. Smooth the ice cream with a metal spatula and add a little extra melted chocolate here and there if necessary. Refrigerate for 10 minutes before serving. Each half makes 1 portion.

Variations: For Iced Strawberry Molds, replace the fudge and cream mixture with chopped fresh or frozen strawberries. For miniature Tutti-Frutti Bombes, replace fudge mixture with 2 ounces each of chopped toasted hazelnuts and rinsed chopped glacé cherries. Containers of different shapes and sizes can be used.

Blackberry Bombe

6 portions

- **1½ cups Blackberry Ice Cream (see Index)**
- **½ cup Bombe Mixture (see Index)**
- **2 tablespoons fresh blackberries**
- **1 teaspoon orange juice**
- **1 teaspoon lemon juice**
- **1 teaspoon grated orange rind**
- **2 tablespoons heavy cream**
- **2 cups fresh blackberries, for garnish**

Make the blackberry ice cream and freeze it. Beat the frozen ice cream with a whisk or wooden spoon until soft enough to be workable. Use it to line the inside of a well-chilled 2-cup bombe mold. Cover and freeze until ice cream is very hard.

Cook the bombe mixture following the step-by-step instructions and allow it to cool. Sort the blackberries, remove any hulls or leaves, wash quickly and drain well. Put the berries in a small bowl. Pour in the fruit juices, add the grated orange rind, and toss gently. Whip the cream lightly. Fold cream and the blackberry and juice mixture into the cooled bombe mixture. Turn the bombe mixture into the mold lined with the ice cream and level the top with a spatula. Cover, overwrap the mold, and label it. Freeze, and store in the freezer for 2 hours to 3 months.

To serve, remove wrappings and lid. Wrap the mold in a cloth and dip into hot water. Unmold on a plate, then smooth the surface of the ice cream. Put the unmolded bombe back in the freezer for a few minutes to make the outside firm if any of it has melted during the unmolding. Place uncovered in the refrigerator for 15 minutes before serving. Decorate with a border of fresh blackberries, washed and well drained.

Apricot Ice Cream

8 portions

- **1 pound dried apricots**
- **¼ cup granulated sugar**
- **3 cups light cream**
- **1 vanilla bean, or 1 teaspoon vanilla extract**
- **2 egg yolks**
- **¼ cup superfine granulated sugar**
- **1 cup heavy cream**
- **1 tablespoon apricot brandy**

Cover the apricots with twice their volume of cold water. Add the granulated sugar, bring to a boil, cover, and simmer for 40 minutes. Remove from the heat. Leave the apricots in the covered pan to soak for 5 hours.

Pour the light cream into a heavy saucepan and scald it. Add the vanilla bean, cover, and leave to infuse for 15 minutes.

Put the egg yolks into the top pan of a double boiler, add the superfine sugar, and beat with a wooden spoon. Remove the vanilla bean from the hot cream and pour the cream onto the eggs in a thin trickle, stirring continuously. Fill the bottom pan of the double boiler with hot water and set the top over it. Cook gently, stirring continuously, without allowing the water underneath to boil. The custard should take about 15 minutes to cook. When cooked, it will coat the back of a spoon. Add vanilla extract if you are using it. Cool, then chill the custard.

Drain the apricots and purée them in a blender or food processor. Stir the apricot purée into the cold custard mixture. Turn the mixture into an ice-cube tray, loaf pan or bowl. Cover and freeze to a mush, about 2 hours.

Whip the heavy cream until it forms soft peaks. Remove ice cream from the freezer and beat it briskly. Stir in the whipped cream and the brandy. Return ice cream to the freezer tray, cover, and refreeze for 1½ hours longer.

Remove ice cream from the freezer and beat once more. Return to the container, cover, and freeze until firm.

Fruit and Nut Ice Cream

6 portions

1 cup milk
4 tablespoons honey
2 large eggs
2 extra egg yolks
1½ teaspoons grated nutmeg
1 cup heavy cream
4 ounces seedless dried fruits (raisins, golden raisins, currants)
4 tablespoons chopped almonds or hazelnuts

Pour the milk into a small heavy pan. Add the honey and scald the mixture. Beat the whole eggs and extra egg yolks in the top pan of a double boiler. Pour the hot milk and honey into the eggs in a thin trickle, stirring continuously with a wooden spoon. Fill the bottom pan of the double boiler with hot water and set the top pan over it; do not allow the water underneath to boil. Cook the custard gently, stirring until it thickens. This will take about 15 minutes. The custard is cooked when it coats the back of the spoon. Strain custard into a bowl and add the nutmeg. Cool, then chill the custard.

Pour the custard into a freezer tray, loaf pan or bowl. Cover, and freeze for 45 minutes, until mushy. Beat the heavy cream to soft peaks. Remove frozen mixture from the freezer and stir to remove ice crystals. Stir in the cream. Return to the container and freeze for 45 minutes longer.

Remove the ice cream from the freezer and beat it once more. Add the dried fruits and chopped nuts, and stir in. Return to the container and cover; freeze until firm.

Iced Turinois

12 portions

1 pint Chocolate Ice Cream (see Index)
1 cup heavy cream
2 large egg whites
1 cup sweetened chestnut purée
whipped cream (optional)
marrons glacés or grated chocolate (optional)

Beat the ice cream to soften it a little and use it to line a chilled cake pan. Be careful to press the ice cream firmly into the corners where the base joins the sides of the pan. Cover with wax paper and foil and freeze for 1½ hours. This freezing time is longer than usual because the ice-cream layer is extra thick.

Whip the cream. Beat the egg whites until stiff. Sieve the chestnut purée and fold it into the whipped cream. Then fold the mixture into the egg whites. Turn the mixture into the center of the frozen ice cream, pressing it down firmly. Level the top, cover, and freeze again, this time for 3 hours.

Uncover the mold, wrap it in a cloth, dip it into hand-hot water, and turn out on a plate. Smooth the surface with a spatula and refrigerate the cake for 15 to 20 minutes before serving. If you wish, decorate the cake with a border of whipped cream and put a few whole *marrons glacés* or a sprinkling of grated chocolate in the center of the top.

Variation: For Midsummer Special, use a scant 1½ cups strawberry ice cream for the first layer. Immediately line it with a single layer of whole raspberries, pressing them firmly into the ice-cream wall. Cover and freeze for 1 hour. Then fill with a bombe mixture flavored with chopped fresh strawberries or whole red currants and a little grated orange rind. Decorate with fresh summer fruits and/or whipped cream just before serving.

Strawberry Ice Cream

4 portions

1 pint strawberries
1¾ cups confectioners' sugar
juice of ½ orange
juice of ½ lemon
1 cup heavy cream

Wash and hull the strawberries, and chop them. Sift the confectioners' sugar into a bowl. Purée the strawberries in a blender or food processor. Strain to remove the seeds. Measure out 1 cup of the strawberry purée and stir it into the sieved confectioners' sugar. Add the orange and lemon juices to the purée. Chill the purée in the refrigerator.

Beat the cream to soft peaks. Fold cream into the fruit purée and turn over until the cream and fruit are mixed. Pour mixture into a freezer tray, loaf pan or bowl. Cover with foil and freeze for 45 minutes.

Remove freezer tray and turn the partly frozen mush into a bowl. Stir thoroughly, turning the frozen outsides into the softer middle. Return to the freezer tray and freeze for 45 minutes longer.

Turn out the frozen ice cream and stir vigorously once more to break up ice crystals. Return ice cream to the freezer. After 45 minutes it will be ready for serving. Remove ice cream from the freezer 20 minutes before serving to allow it to soften slightly.

Variations: Make Blackberry Ice Cream by substituting blackberries for the strawberries. Add 2 teaspoons kirsch liqueur. Substitute chopped peaches for the strawberries to make Peach Ice Cream. Add 1 teaspoon almond extract. Make Raspberry Ice Cream by substituting raspberries for the strawberries.

Part Five
PAELLA FIESTA

Relaxation and conviviality are the keynotes of a paella fiesta. This is a well-seasoned, hearty meal, redolent of garlic, saffron and other pungent herbs and spices, all guaranteed to stimulate the senses and make the conversation flow and sparkle. Enjoy this party in casual surroundings— an outdoor patio, around a kitchen table, beside a bonfire on the beach or by the open hearth—and in the company of friends who like to laugh and talk and linger over a rustic spread of food and wine. Best of all, the entire menu is one that is improved by being prepared well ahead, leaving only half an hour or so for final cooking.

The meal begins with a bowl of iced white gazpacho to refresh and stimulate even the most jaded palate. This delicious soup is a pleasing variation on the more familiar tomato-based gazpacho. As it is served well chilled, it must be made some hours in advance, preferably the day before. Under no circumstances should this creamy soup be relegated to summer only. It makes a surprising and pleasant beginning to a dinner on a winter evening.

The crusty, French-style loaves of homemade bread are welcome at any meal; they are not difficult to make. This dough, like many other yeast doughs, can be shaped into loaves and frozen before baking, or can be baked, cooled, and stored in the freezer for almost instant future use.

Paella, with its vivid colors and mélange of textures and tastes, is perfect party food. The presentation is impressive and the dish is a sure-fire crowd pleaser. Although the preparation of a paella requires a number of steps, they are all simple and almost all can be done well in advance. The final assembly need take no longer than half an hour. The paella can then rest for up to twenty minutes, while you enjoy a bowl of cold gazpacho.

Paella pans, made of metal, are equipped with handles on each side. They are the most suitable pans for cooking and serving paella. If you lack one, a large iron skillet or even a sauté pan of ample size can make an adequate substitute. The recipe for paella that follows is intended to be cooked indoors, first on a conventional stovetop, then in an oven, but the adventurous at heart can transport the entire meal into the out-of-doors and the paella can be cooked over a wood or charcoal fire, as is often done in Spain. (If paella becomes one of your favorite company dishes, you may wish to buy a gas burner ring made especially to fit the paella pan. By providing more uniform and controllable heat, the ring facilitates the making of a fine paella.)

Paella, with its glorious mix of briny clams, mussels and shrimps, the robust flavors of marinated chicken and spicy sausage, all nestled in a bed of saffron rice, is a wholly satisfying one-dish meal. There is no need to prepare any complicated side dishes to enhance it. A bowl of hot and spicy garlic sauce with its red ripe tomatoes and refreshing tangy herbs is passed separately to add piquancy to the rich flavors of the paella.

Sangría, made with a dry, full-bodied wine, accented with the sharp flavors of citrus and the natural sweetness of fresh fruit, the whole made effervescent with the addition of sparkling water, is the perfect thirst-quenching beverage to accompany this meal.

Dessert is a lemon-flavored ice cream, made with an egg-yolk custard base, in the European style. It should be made two or three days in advance. The almond-flavored macaroons, an old-fashioned treat that perfectly complements the delectable ice cream, conveniently use the remaining egg whites; these should be made ahead as well.

This meal calls for rustic table decorations—rough woven baskets, colorful pottery bowls, plates and even goblets (no need for anything to match), masses of flowers gathered from the fields, or baskets filled with fruits in season. Bright vivid colors recalling Spanish hillsides and fiestas should echo the colors of the foods. Make everything ahead, relax, then join the party as your own guest.

PAELLA FIESTA

A Relaxed, Informal Dinner for 12 Hearty Eaters

Iced White Gazpacho
Homemade Loaves of Crusty Bread
Shellfish, Chicken and Sausage Paella
with
Spicy Garlic Sauce
Lemon Velvet Ice Cream
and
Almond Macaroons
Beverage: Sangría

MARKET LIST

Meat and Fish

- 4 whole chicken breasts
- 1½ pounds sweet Italian sausage or Spanish chorizo sausage
- 3 dozen mussels
- 3 dozen Little Neck clams
- 1½ pounds shrimps

Fruits and Vegetables

- 2 oranges
- 10 lemons
- your choice of ripe peaches, apples, strawberries or raspberries (to garnish the sangría)
- 1 head of garlic
- 2 medium-size cucumbers
- 2 large green peppers
- 1 bunch of scallions
- 1 bunch of parsley
- 1 bunch of basil
- 1 shallot
- 1 large onion
- 1 package (10 ounces) frozen peas
- 1 jar or can (4 or 5 ounces) pimientos
- 2 large ripe tomatoes
- 1 can (28 ounces) imported plum tomatoes
- 2 cups blanched almonds

Staples

- frozen orange juice
- white bread
- eggs
- olive oil
- sugar
- chicken broth (12 cups)
- heavy cream (3 cups)
- salt
- coarse salt
- white pepper
- black pepper
- cayenne pepper
- ground saffron
- bay leaf
- dried thyme
- dried coriander
- dried red pepper flakes
- dry yeast (1 envelope)
- unbleached flour
- yellow corn meal
- rice (round-grain Arborio, if possible)
- milk
- cornstarch
- vanilla extract
- almond extract

Other

- dry red wine
- seltzer or club soda
- orange liqueur, such as Grand Marnier or Cointreau
- dry white wine or dry vermouth

A Word about Sangría

Sangría, the Spanish word for "bleeding," and referring no doubt to the blood-red color of the wine, originated in Spain and is said to have been introduced to this country in 1964 in the Spanish Pavilion at the New York World's Fair. It gained instant and wide-reaching popularity as a light and refreshing party drink and eventually inspired the commercial manufacture of a prepared sangría drink. Perhaps because of this commercialization, it fell into disfavor for a while, but this was a great loss. A well-made sangría, preferably using one of the full-bodied, dry red wines of the Rioja district of Spain—for example Viña Vial, Solar de Samaniego, Campo Viejo or Viña Pomal—is a refreshing and delicious drink. Although it is most commonly served as a cooling beverage in summertime, it can be served to advantage at other times, whenever the menu calls for a light, full-flavored drink that can be quaffed instead of sipped.

Although white-wine sangría does not exist in Spain, it too can be delicious and a wonderful alternative to a spritzer.

Sangría

about 24 portions

- **2 oranges**
- **2 lemons**
- **1 peach or 1 apple, or ½ cup sliced strawberries or whole raspberries**
- **2 bottles dry red wine, preferably imported from Spain**
- **2 tablespoons undiluted frozen orange juice**
- **½ cup orange liqueur, such as Grand Marnier or Cointreau**
- **1 bottle (28 ounces) seltzer or club soda**

Cut oranges and lemons into thin slices and remove any seeds. Slice the peach or apple, if you are using either. Mix all ingredients except seltzer or club soda in a large pitcher or punch bowl. Refrigerate for several hours or overnight.

Add seltzer or club soda and ice cubes just before serving. Have a ladle or large spoon handy to add some fruit to each serving.

Variation: Substitute dry white wine for a delicious white-wine version.

Iced White Gazpacho

12 portions

- **6 cups chicken stock**
- **2 cucumbers**
- **2 green peppers**
- **3 garlic cloves**
- **4 scallions**
- **6 slices of white bread**
- **2 eggs**
- **6 tablespoons olive oil**
- **½ teaspoon sugar**
- **¼ cup lemon juice**
- **1 cup heavy cream**
- **salt and white pepper**

Chill the chicken stock and remove all fat from the surface. Peel and seed cucumbers. Wash peppers and halve them; discard stems, seeds and ribs. Cut cucumbers and peppers into ½-inch chunks. Peel garlic cloves. Wash and trim scallions, chop them, wrap in plastic, and refrigerate until serving time.

Remove crusts from bread and soak bread in cold water, then squeeze with your hands to remove as much moisture as possible. Break eggs into the bowl of a food processor and process until color turns pale. With processor on, pour in the olive oil in a thin stream. Add soaked bread, garlic cloves, cucumbers, peppers, sugar and lemon juice. Process until smooth. (The soup may also be made in a blender.)

Pour the vegetable mixture into a large bowl and add the chilled chicken stock. Stir until well mixed. Stir in the heavy cream. Season with salt and pepper to taste. Refrigerate for several hours or overnight.

Serve in cold bowls, garnished with the chopped scallions.

Spicy Garlic Sauce

makes about 2½ cups

- 3 garlic cloves
- 1 teaspoon coarse salt
- ½ teaspoon dried red pepper flakes, or to taste
- ½ cup olive oil
- 2 large ripe tomatoes, or 1½ cups well-drained canned tomatoes
- ½ cup minced fresh parsley
- ½ cup minced fresh basil (optional)
- juice of 1 lemon
- black pepper
- broth from paella, or water

Peel the garlic cloves; in a mortar, with a pestle, crush them together with the salt to a fine paste. Add the pepper flakes and beat in the olive oil. Transfer to a medium-size bowl. Peel and chop tomatoes. Add tomatoes, parsley, basil, lemon juice and freshly ground black pepper to taste. If sauce is very thick, moisten with some broth from the paella or with a little water. Taste for seasoning and adjust as needed. The sauce should be sharp and spicy. Let it stand at room temperature for several hours. Pass the sauce at table to garnish the paella.

Shellfish, Chicken and Sausage Paella

12 portions

- 3 garlic cloves
- ½ teaspoon dried thyme
- ½ teaspoon ground coriander
- ¼ teaspoon cayenne pepper
- juice of 1 lemon
- 4 chicken breasts
- 1½ pounds sweet Italian sausage or Spanish chorizo sausage
- 1½ cups dry white wine or water or dry vermouth
- 3 dozen mussels
- 3 dozen Little Neck clams
- 2 or 3 sprigs of parsley
- 1 shallot
- 1 bay leaf
- 1½ pounds shrimps in shells
- 1 large onion
- 2 cups canned plum tomatoes
- 3 canned pimientos
- ¼ cup olive oil
- 3 cups uncooked rice, preferably short-grain Arborio
- ½ teaspoon ground saffron
- 5 to 6 cups chicken stock
- 1 package (10 ounces) frozen peas
- black pepper
- lemon wedges, for garnish
- Spicy Garlic Sauce (preceding recipe)

Peel and mince the garlic. Mix garlic, thyme, coriander, cayenne and lemon juice together in a bowl. Skin and bone the chicken breasts and cut into bite-size pieces. Add chicken to marinade, tossing pieces around so all are evenly coated. Let them stand in the refrigerator for several hours or overnight.

Place the sausage and 1 cup of the wine in a heavy skillet; prick sausage with a fork in several places. Cook, covered, over moderate heat for 30 minutes. Turn sausage once about halfway through. Remove sausage and let it cool. Slice sausage into thin rounds. Skim fat from the liquid remaining in the skillet, and reserve the liquid.

Scrub and debeard the mussels, and scrub the clams well. Wash parsley. Peel and mince the shallot. Pour remaining ½ cup wine into a large pot. Add parsley, shallot, bay leaf, clams and mussels. Cover and steam over moderate heat until all shellfish are open. Discard any that do not open. Let everything cool. Remove clams and mussels from the broth, and reserve. Strain broth through several layers of dampened cheesecloth to remove any sand, and reserve broth also.

Shell and devein the shrimps. Peel and mince the onion. Drain both tomatoes and pimientos. Chop tomatoes and slice pimientos. Sauté minced onion in the olive oil in a large paella pan, large skillet or sauté pan. When onion begins to color, add marinated chicken pieces and stir-fry for a few minutes. Add the rice and stir with a wooden spoon over low heat for about 5 minutes. The rice should be evenly coated with oil and the kernels should turn opaque. Stir in chopped tomatoes and sliced sausage. Sprinkle with saffron.

Combine the reserved sausage poaching liquid, the strained shellfish broth, and enough of the chicken broth to make 7 cups. Heat it. Add 6 cups of the hot broth to the rice and cook over medium-high heat, stirring occasionally, until liquid is almost all absorbed, about 15 minutes. Turn the peas into a strainer and let them thaw.

Preheat oven to 350°F. Remove paella pan from heat. Stir peas and shrimps into the rice and sausage. Tuck the opened clams and mussels, still in their shells, all over the paella. Garnish with pimiento slices. Moisten shellfish with some of the remaining broth. Slide paella pan into the oven for 10 minutes to heat through. Remove from oven and cover with a heavy absorbent towel until ready to serve. The paella can wait this way for up to 20 minutes.

Grind fresh black pepper over the paella and garnish with lemon wedges just before serving. Pass the Spicy Garlic Sauce separately.

Crusty Bread

makes 2 long loaves

- **1 envelope active dry yeast, 1 scant tablespoon**
- **½ teaspoon sugar**
- **1¼ cups warm water, 105° to 115°F**
- **3 cups unbleached flour**
- **2 teaspoons salt**
- **additional flour as needed**
- **oil for bowl**
- **3 tablespoons yellow corn meal**

Dissolve the yeast and sugar in the warm water. Let stand until foamy. In a large bowl, mix flour and salt with a wooden spoon. Make a well in the center of the flour and pour in the yeast mixture. Mix well with the wooden spoon, then turn out on a floured surface. Knead for 10 to 15 minutes, adding more flour if necessary, until dough is no longer sticky. Place dough in an oiled large bowl and cover with a towel. Let stand for about 2 hours, until doubled in bulk.

Punch down dough and turn it out on the floured board. Knead for 5 minutes more, then divide dough into 2 equal parts. Shape each part into a long, French-style loaf. Place loaves on a baking sheet that has been sprinkled with cornmeal. Cut diagonal slits in the tops of the loaves in several places. Cover with a towel and let rise for another hour.

Preheat oven to 425°F. Spray loaves of bread with water from an atomizer, and place them in the oven. Wait 5 minutes, then spray loaves again so that oven becomes steamy. Bake for 15 minutes, until bread is brown and crusty and has a hollow sound when tapped on the bottom.

Serve warm or cool, but serve on the same day as baked, unless you freeze the loaves.

Lemon Velvet Ice Cream

makes 1½ quarts

- **4 egg yolks**
- **¾ cup sugar**
- **2 cups milk**
- **2 cups heavy cream**
- **grated rind of 2 lemons**
- **¼ cup lemon juice**

Beat egg yolks together with the sugar until mixture becomes very pale and thick. Pour milk and cream into a heavy saucepan. Add grated lemon rind to the saucepan and heat until hot but not simmering. Beat half of the hot milk and cream by a tablespoonful at a time into the egg yolks. Pour warmed egg-yolk mixture into the balance of the milk and cream and mix. Cook over low heat, stirring constantly, until custard thickens and almost simmers. Let custard cool and refrigerate for several hours or overnight.

Stir lemon juice into the custard and pour custard into a freezer container. Cover with foil and freeze for 45 minutes or until mushy. Turn ice cream into bowl and beat thoroughly. Cover and return to freezer until at mushy stage again, about 45 minutes. Remove from freezer and once more beat thoroughly. Return ice cream to freezer until frozen. Alternatively, the ice cream can be made in an ice-cream machine frozen according to manufacturer's instruction.

Ice cream will develop better flavor if allowed to rest in the freezer for a day or two before serving.

Almond Macaroons

makes 2 dozen

- **2 cups blanched almonds**
- **1 cup sugar**
- **2 tablespoons cornstarch**
- **4 egg whites**
- **½ teaspoon vanilla extract**
- **½ teaspoon almond extract**

Preheat oven to 350°F. Line 2 baking sheets with aluminum foil. Grind almonds in a food processor or nut grinder to a fine powder. Mix ground almonds, sugar and cornstarch together in a large bowl. Beat egg whites until stiff but not dry, adding vanilla and almond extracts at end of beating. Fold egg whites into ground almond and sugar mixture. Drop by tablespoon onto the baking sheets, or use a pastry bag to squeeze out half-dollar-size mounds. Leave 1½ to 2 inches between the mounds. Bake for about 20 minutes, until macaroons turn a delicate golden brown. Cool on a rack.

Macaroons will dry out quickly and should be eaten within 2 or 3 days.

INDEX